The Other King

What the Animals, Trees, Crystals, Angels, E.T.s, Mermaids and Fairies Had to Say

Helena Hawley

The Other Kingdoms Speak

What the Animals, Trees, Crystals, Angels, E.T.s, Mermaids and Fairies Had to Say

ISBN 186163 062 X

Cover and internal illustrations by Helena Hawley
Cover design by Paul Mason

Published by:

Capall Bann Publishing
Freshfields
Chieveley
Berks
RG20 8TF

I dedicate this book to the animals, the fairies, the mermaids, the angels, and the trees; all of whom have done so much to enhance my life.

Acknowledgements

I wish to acknowledge the help, moral support, and advice of Linda Tellington-Jones, as without her assistance I could never have written this book in its present form.

I am also thankful for the encouragement of Chris Griscom with my paintings, and the benefits I received from my Light Institute sessions.

I thank both my late mother and Jill Robinson who painstakingly corrected my spelling and punctuation.

Contents

Preface

This is a lonely planet. Alone in its illusion that it stands in the abyss of space, where no intelligence, no life force, no companion, is available to teach or comfort as it moves forward on its eternal journey to some illusive goal. We humans, viewing ourselves as the highest species and stewards of this lonely planet, have almost lost our evolutionary passage into wholeness through the tenacity of our conclusion that we, alone, have the intelligence to make the decisions that shape our world. Yet, ever so gently, the other sentient species who dwell with us on physical and non-physical planes are attempting to break through our barriers and deliver us from the folly of our self-imposed isolationism.

The mark of our loneliness has become painfully visible around the planet. It is being expressed by individuals, whole societies and nations of humans who are seeking some new experience of home, of connectedness to source. It seems that only the child in each of us retains a distant memory of communion with other than the human form. The child in its divine equality can speak to the rocks and the plants, the insects and all the animals, feeling it to be a personal relationship that comforts and entertains and guides. Other beings do not judge worth by a narrow span of mental intelligence, but rather accept as of great value the intelligence of the heart.

For children, the communication with animals has more to do with companionship and comfort for the gentle soul in such a strange world as this. Each tender child experiences psychic communication with many forms of living beings including angels, devas and space beings and is therefore enriched by cosmic perception and the capacity to receive higher knowing.

Helena Hawley's exquisite book "*The Other Kingdoms Speak*", opens the floodgates to our hearts, our minds, and our memories.

It is a book to inspire and to stir deep within all humans, the realisation of our capacity to commune with the other species who share our planetary reality. Through her magnificent psychic gifts we are given a great and important teaching which is that not only can the animals speak, but when they speak, they reveal to us our true purpose. They plead for us to remember that as the stewards of this planet, we must become aware of how we have endangered them, and return to a harmonic relationship if our world is to make the catapoltic leap into the light frequencies of cosmic dimensions.

This book is an essential stepping stone for those who would remember their place in the universe. Helena tells her story in such a straight-forward style, that she endears herself to us as we feel we are moving around in her life with her. It is a journey from hopeless separation to the pressing awareness that she is part of a bigger whole to which she can give a meaningful assistance. Her powerful breakthrough into self awareness allows us, as well, to feel an upliftment of our own sense of value. It is clear that the voices of the animals come from their beautiful spirit, not at all from some inner need for emotional comfort, but from a place of exquisite dignity and truth. As they have trusted her capacity to speak for them, we trust her as well and feel the honour bestowed upon her to carry forth the messages of the animals. They begin, as in all good teachings, to shed light on individual awareness so that she can clear away her personal karmic realities and enter into a higher vibrational level without distortion or personal veils.

Helena has integrated meditation as a part of her daily expression. Her profound relationship with mother nature triggers a longing to find that same intimacy ourselves. It is very inspiring for the reader to enter with her into those peaceful altered states that become the windows to the interspecies communication. Most of the animals who speak to Helena are "wild animals" who eloquently share the realities of their struggle to coexist with us. They are wise and patient and yet stimulate the hungry cry of our own psyche to live again the freedom and excitement that they represent to us. The wild animal is to our spirit as the domestic is to our emotions.

We humans tend to project our emotions onto the animals we call pets and so influence their psyche that they do, indeed, take on human characteristics. We talk to them and are sure that they understand what we say, but rarely do we ever consider that they may have something to relate to us! The messages from the animals to Helena are touching yet simple. They speak to us in our terms and about mutual problems. They bring us a sense of wonderment that these beings do indeed share with us, not only our planet, but in some strange way, even our consciousness.

Helena's description of "The Council of the Animals" is electrifying in its revelation that not only do individual animals reach through the barriers of diverse species, but that whole groups can gather to review collective situations! In the face of such a possibility, we must ponder if there is not some profound and helpful learning to take place if we could bridge the gap of *consciousness and hear what they are discussing. After all, the* dolphins have been on the planet two million years longer than us, and it is possible that instead of being the superior species, we might be their "little brothers." The grasshoppers can produce an enzyme that protects them from radiation. Perhaps we should ask them about this before our genetic material is endangered by the present increases of radiation on the planet. It is very important that we realise the innate intelligence of each and all species and begin to seek out the wisdom that is vital to our global living community.

The image of the Council of Animals harkens back to the ancient myths which told of peace throughout the land when "the lion lay down with the lamb" and prophecies that promised the possibility of peace in some distant future. It is breathtaking to contemplate how other species are now engaged in dialogue that we humans have not been able to embrace. Through the aid of people like Miss Hawley, we must join in and hear what the infinite "others" are talking about. It is disconcerting that much of what the animals have to discuss is about how we humans are destroying the delicate balance on our planet. It is not too late to repair the damage and recreate a new existence of harmony with the help of our brothers the animals.

The great books that have been recorded from the dawn of history tell us legends of beings that walked our earth in the form of gods. They all had telepathic and psychic powers which they used to convey teaching to all living forms. We must return to these capacities of telepathic, psychic and spiritual communication in order to fulfil human destiny. It is an echo entrapped in our blood crystals, walled within ancient DNA molecules of the origins of our own celestial bodies. We humans are at last re-awakening from a deathly sleep and remembering what has been lost from the times before Atlantis when we could speak to all sentient beings.

During the time of Atlantis when the male and female were divided and genetic engineering created odd and imbalanced species, we lost our higher capacities and entered into an extended epic of darkness and doubt. Our DNA is so filled with trepidation from the struggle of one species and even one tribe against another, that it is difficult for us to be willing to surrender our defensive separation enough to become psychically attuned to anything outside ourselves.

There have always been those who have maintained these capacities even within the shadows of our constant upheavals and the willingness to admit that we have such fantastic abilities is renewing our sense of pride in the human species. The light of consciousness is persistent and we will come once again to the shores of unlimited potential. We will claim what was once a natural part of humanness: to be totally psychic, to hear the heart of any living being and by communicating who we are, to remember again the joy and ecstasy that belongs to us.

Here is where our friends in the animal kingdom are to be of great service to us. Because of the mistrust for the negative nuances of our own cultures, it is easier and in a way more urgent for us to communicate psychically with our animal brothers. By realising that we can be telepathic with the animal kingdom, we can return to the openness of our childlike qualities that pull away the veil of physical and dimensional confusion.

Helena Hawley is one of the first to speak with the mermaids and enlighten us as to their true nature. The realisation that we can interact with them may have great relevance to our understanding of the mighty oceans that cover 80% of this planet. We desperately need to learn about the sea and its place of balance in the planetary scenario. The mermaids can become our teachers and guide us into a new octave of relationship with this primordial home from which we fled so many eons ago. Under the tutelage of the mermaids as sea spirits, in the same way that the plant spirits or devas guard the vegetable kingdom, we can perhaps contribute to the harmony of all. There is no doubt that the health of our oceans will play a crucial role in the future well-being of all earth's inhabitants.

Communication with the animal spirits, fairies, and mermaids amplifies our recognition of the living force inherent in all dimensions and worlds that are impinging upon our own. Strengthened by the gratitude of experiencing a larger whole, we may again allow ourselves to acknowledge that we are forever inextricably connected to each other and that we can trust our compassionate intuitive knowing of what is going on deep within the others around us. Let us return with new commitment and love to our gardens, our seas, our soul friends and spirits, the animals.

I am deeply grateful to Helena Hawley for having given the world this book. I have been enthralled by the powerful heart energy extended from the animals and the spirits of their beings. Their consciousness and profound wisdom is a gift to us all. I found Helena's drawings so wonderful that I had to touch them again and again to feel the exquisite vibration that comes right through the medium to the paper. She is a consummate artist and channel.

With great love,

Chris Griscom

Introduction

I am writing this book in order to share what I have been given. It is with much joy that I am passing on some of the communications that I have received from the animal and other non-human kingdoms. I am certainly not the first person to have had such experiences, but nonetheless I find these happenings as valuable evidence that such things do happen when we allow *them to, and therefore they should be shared.*

At first, I had the idea that only the animal communications should be published, and that it would be entirely superfluous to include anything about myself at all. Even if the animals had told me to do so, I think that I still would not have done it. However, they spoke to my good friend Linda Tellington-Jones, who does so much for them,and she passed it on to me that they really wanted me to reveal myself in this book. I can see now that doing so will make it all seem more real to those who read it.

I am able to tell a little of how it was for me, when I was very young indeed due to spontaneous flash-backs, which have allowed me to re-experience things which I would otherwise have no memory of. Some of my story I can put together thanks to information from people who knew me at the time, and most of it simply from my own memories.

My first memory starts when I was still a baby. I was so minute, that I felt that my mother held me more in her hands than in her arms, although it was probably some of both. I had no words, and limited sight. I realised that the person holding me found me a novelty, and that she enjoyed looking at my tiny features and limbs. During this thorough examination from my mother, I felt as though I was in my seventh heaven, as I experienced the feel of her hands and fingers, sometimes directly, and sometimes through whatever material I was wrapped in. I lay there fascinated by the different sensations that I could experience from the touch of another human being, so different from what one felt from physical contact with the sides of my cot, for example. I was enjoying being physical, and still felt in touch with love, and who I was. This was to be a happy and content phase of my life.

As I grew older, my connection to the unseen worlds became less conscious. Therefore I was increasingly more dependent on the love of those around me to help me feel secure. The arrival of a sister two years younger than me naturally diverted much of the attention away from me. I was no longer so secure, and this was when I became moody and difficult.

By then, I had no idea why I was in the World, or where I had come from. I only knew that I wanted to be loved, and constantly reassured that I was the only thing that mattered. Instead, very soon I was told that I should learn to be unselfish, which seemed to mean giving away things that I wanted to keep. Therefore I remained selfish. I never lacked warm clothes, or things to eat, or toys to play with, but like many children, I craved more attention. I was a natural daydreamer, like many others with psychic ability, but I had to learn early on that if, for example, I saw a patch of blue colour drifting about under the chest of drawers in my bedroom, it was better not to say anything about it. When I did, I remember being told not to be so stupid. "Of course there is nothing there. You must be overtired, so get into bed, and go to sleep." This was how I discovered, that not everyone could see everything that I saw.

One sunny afternoon, I walked out onto the lawn, and found my little sister sleeping in her pram. I peeped over the side of the pram, and looked at her. I understood that she was the reason for my world not being how I wanted it to be, but what could I do about it? She had invaded my environment, and I was filled with a feeling of hopelessness and helplessness, as I knew of nothing that I could do that would change anything for me. She was unavoidably there. I was far too young to wonder how it must be for her.

I resented being expected to grow up. To me it meant growing away from love. The more independent I became, the less things were done for me, and the less I felt loved. My little sister had the advantage it seemed that she was *still* young enough for my mother to take her on her lap. When I asked for the same treatment, I was told that I was too old. Not knowing how to make myself any younger, I had to go without. I had a nanny who was fairly physical, but my mother seemed to have been brought up to keep everyone at a good arms length whenever possible. I felt rejection, and this was not to be the last time.

I started day-school aged about five. It did not please me. I much preferred playing the games of my imagination in the garden at home. I disliked being asked to use my brain, and refused to make any effort with writing, reading, or arithmetic. Fortunately my mother explained to me that if I grew up unable to do these things when everyone else could, then I would always be laughed at. This sounded such a severe threat, that I began to try a little bit, and actually quite enjoyed it when I became proficient enough to be able to read children's stories. By that time I was a year older than most of the other people in my class. Backward they call it. The next outlet for my psychic ability was simply using a powerful imagination to construct scenarios which I could act out together with my friends at day-school. I was usually the star in these. This I see as a normal behaviour pattern amongst children, most of whom learn to suppress it later in life. Usually it is lost automatically during the process of formal education, most of which only develops the analytical thinking side of the brain.

At nine, I was sent away to boarding school, where my intuitive side was once again in action, as I became a popular story-teller, simply by recounting some of the experiences that I was having on the astral plane, or from past-life memories that sometimes came floating back to me. I remember the other children asking me, "Have you ever known anyone like that?" or "Where on earth do you get these stories from?" At the time I could only say that I found everything in my head. "They just come out of my head," I would say. I could not have told them any more, but I do remember feeling uncomfortable about this account of it without knowing why.

I had no idea that my psychic senses were developed more than many. I was growing up in an environment where such things were never mentioned. As is often the case with children, I had a strong fascination for fairies, angels, elves, gnomes, witches, and ghosts. Again, like many people, as I became engulfed by the hard world of adults and education, I lost most of my intuition. The psychic senses simply closed down.

One would think that that would have enabled me to fit very neatly into society, but that was not always the case. I had not been at boarding school that long, before there were whisperings going round the school that maybe I was not quite right in the head. Finally, one day it was admitted openly amongst the other girls that I was mad. This was a terrible label to wear. Nobody wanted to be seen anywhere near me for fear of being teased by the others for playing with someone who was crazy. After a while, one or two people did seem to be talking to me again, but the damage was done. I was now afraid of letting anyone really get to know me in case they decided that I was even crazier than I was already thought to be. Desperate for some kind of acceptance, or the possibility of some belief in myself, I asked one or two of the teachers in the school if they thought that I was crazy. "No, you are not mad," they would tell me, but with over seventy girls in the school, I could not see how so many of them could really be wrong.

The effect of this on me was that I spent more and more time playing alone. I was also a person who the other children took great delight in teasing unmercifully. I would get upset very easily, which made it great fun for them. My grandmother tried to comfort me by telling me that those who get teased a lot often turn into very nice people, and she advised me to try and avoid letting anyone see how much it upset me, as it would be dull for them if I did not react. When I mastered that, I must admit that it did help. However, I had no such solution for my other problem, and therefore I found that just being in my own company was a great relief. It felt like a successful escape from a swarm of biting mosquitoes. I never understood how I could get on better with people, or why they thought that I was mad. (As you will read further on in this book, I did eventually find out why, but that was over thirty years later.) At the time, I often thought that if I only knew what I did that made me appear mad, then I could try and change my behaviour, and become accepted. However, I was getting progressively less fond of people, so I retreated inwards, and turned to art and music for pleasure and self-expression.

One wonderful thing did happen in my life. My parents bought a pony. Ponies are simply wonderful, as no one has ever taught them that there is any difference between the sane and the insane. They quite simply take you as they find you. When I felt that the rest of the world had turned against me, and made me feel like an outcast, I found that a pony was just as ready to take a carrot from me as from anyone else. No wonder that I hated school, and longed for the school holidays, when I could come home and ride my pony again.

This pony taught me some very useful lessons, and more particularly the following pony who was bought when I outgrew the first one. The second pony was exceptionally nervous, and had obviously undergone some rough and unsympathetic treatment from humans before my parents bought him. The only way that I could get one hundred percent of his co-operation, which took me years, was to handle him with patience and gentleness at all times. For this reason, I learnt to control my wild and sudden temper. It meant more to me to gain the trust of the pony, than to fly into a rage which brought nothing. I learnt that I could achieve my goals faster, if I controlled my emotions.

After my first year at school, the other children seemed to forget their harsh judgement on my mental state, and things were easier for me for a while. However, after four years at this preparatory school, the time had come for me to move on to the senior part of the establishment. This was a shock to me. Instead of being situated in the country, it was in a town. Far worse than that, it brought me into contact with a large number of people who had never met me before. To my dismay, nearly all of them decided that I was mentally ill, and again I did not understand why. I could do nothing about it. I only remember two girls, both in the top form, who said, "Oh no, she's not mad, she's just very absent minded." Probably they had no idea how much I hung on their words. Finding this tiny minority who could accept me as sane, even though they were too old to want to be friends with me, was the greatest source of comfort that I had. I expect that there were others who agreed, but often people are reluctant to speak out against the majority. This time, thank goodness, these judgements did not last as long as they did at preparatory school, so at the end of three years there, I was daring to believe that I was relatively normal.

Unfortunately, I still hated school work. That I had the ability to do better was frequently written on the school reports that were sent to my parents at the end of each term. They also mentioned that I did not mix well with the other girls. This last point must have worried my parents, as they told me that I should mix with the other girls, as it was unfriendly not to; but no one could tell me how to mix with them, and getting me to want to would have been a hopeless task. In spite of poor school reports, I think that some of the staff were able to deduce from my questions and ability to solve problems in class, that I might have a reasonable level of intelligence. Perhaps it was being so spaced out, or my strong addiction to day-dreaming, that made it very hard for me to actually remember anything that we were taught. On the very rare occasions that I really tried to learn something, I found that I could, but only if I had at least three times as much time as everyone else needed for the same work. This meant that my best efforts would never produce enough good work at a time to bring in fair rewards. I quite simply gave up trying for most of the while, because it was like swimming against the tide, and the sea is strong. My parents were concerned about this, and at their request, during a staff meeting my chances of success in the end of school examinations were discussed, and rated as nil.

I suppose that my parents did not want to be left with a brainless incompetent child at the end of my school career, so I was taken away from school, and placed in an establishment where it was hoped that I would receive enough help to pass a few examinations at the end of it. Although I was pleased to leave the school that I did not like, I dreaded going somewhere new, as probably the now familiar rejection on account of my mental state would almost certainly take place. As it turned out, this institution was filled with a variety of misfits, or people who were so badly behaved that their respective schools had expelled them. I think that I was the most normal person there. The only thing that I was constantly teased about was my tendency to wear a skirt most of the time instead of the tight jeans that they wore which nearly cut off the circulation. (In those days, stretch jeans had not been invented.) We were allowed much more freedom than at school, so I used it to go for lovely long walks with one of my misfit type friends, and neither of us did any work. At the end of that year I passed my music and art examinations, but failed everything else. Actually I had only been allowed to try three other subjects, because I was so hopeless. I should add that I had learnt to make a point of being hopeless, as it was the only means I had at my disposal for preventing people from thinking that I ought to be learning even more things that I did not want to bother with. I was unmotivated, and disinterested.

I do not remember ever telling my parents about how mad so many people had decided I was, because as far as I could tell, they thought that I was dim, but sane; and I could not bear to risk giving them any worse ideas about me than that. This little bit of acceptance as a more or less normal individual in my parents' home was very precious to me.

Dismayed by my academic failure, my parents decided to try something else for me. They decided to keep me at home and send me twice a week to a private tutor. I finally managed two more low level examinations in English and history (called 'O' levels). In my opinion, it had very little to do with the private tuition that I was receiving, but instead this small success was due to a clever idea of my mother's. Whereas at school when my work was bad I had been punished, so that almost anything that I did was only motivated by the desire to avoid reprimands, my mother had the brain-wave of saying that if I would agree to work from nine to twelve o'clock each morning, after these three hours I could spend the rest of the day doing whatever I wanted. This meant that as long as I did my personal best each morning, I could spend the afternoons in relative heaven with my pony. I was at last able to work at my own speed in a non-competitive way, and be rewarded for it. Achieving a high grade in the history examination at the end of it showed me that provided that I could work in my own style and time, I was actually capable of learning and remembering information for long enough to sit and pass an examination, even though I could forget it all much faster than I could learn it. Examinations are very often just memory tests. Either you have a memory, or you have not. Many of them have little to do with real intelligence. How true this is of course, must vary from subject to subject, but that is how it seemed to me.

I was very thankful when my academic education came to a close, and I was allowed to embark on a career with horses. My mother had a fairly pessimistic outlook. She said that I was so slow at everything I did, that she could never imagine if I was working as a groom, that I would ever be capable of getting anybody's horse ready for anything on time for them, and therefore I would never be employable. Also her horse-loving friends had told her that horses were very hard work, which is normally true, and I had never shown any inclination to do any work. I think that both parents doubted that I would stick at it for more than a month or two at the most. I begged them to let me try, because the alternative was to become a secretary, which to me meant a condemnation to eternal hell. Worse still, I gathered that one both learnt that and then did it in London, something else that I did not relish.

I hated parties, all social occasions, meeting people, especially strangers, and absolutely anything that kept me away from horses. When my parents had friends in for tea or a drink, I hid myself if possible, usually in the kitchen. My mother complained to me that she was afraid that her friends would think that she treated me like a servant, and would not allow me in the dining room when guests were present. "Also," she went on, "people will start to think that there is something wrong with you if you keep on hiding like this. It is very hard for us to explain it to them." I did not change. I only made 'public appearances' under protest when I simply could not avoid them.

I loved being with horses, and I did not like people. Most people seemed to be pretty false, and as I understood neither myself nor anyone else, it was hardly surprising. When I say 'pretty false', perhaps it is an unfair condemnation, but it is certainly true that other people were much better than I was at knowing how to cope with one another. They seemed to understand perfectly all of the social niceties that I had failed to acquire. For my part, I had not any tact. I never understood what tact was. I simply knew as others had informed me, that it was a necessary quality that was lacking in me. This meant that sooner or later I would put my foot in it, and consequently feel mortally wounded when others backed away from me after such a 'faux pas'.

Although I am a lazy person at times, the hard work in my chosen career was worthwhile to me, as it enabled me to stay with horses. To start with I was definitely a very slow moving groom, but with practice I improved. As I gradually worked my way up, and acquired more qualifications, I found that it was easier to get people to employ me to teach rather than to groom. I therefore found myself rather reluctantly more and more involved in the teaching side of things. I became employed to run yards as 'head girl', or 'chief instructress' etc.. Actually, to some extent this suited me much better. It provided me with a challenge to keep me motivated, and I found that I could run a yard just as fast as anyone else. Being in charge of people was a means of growing up very quickly. This went on for quite some years. By the time that I was thirtyfive, my body was starting to complain about my life-style. I could remember when I was in one of my first jobs at twenty-three years of age thinking "I suppose that I will be capable of doing this kind of physical work until I am about thirty-five, when I will be too old." My body seemed to have made a note of that, and bang on schedule at thirty-five, I started to get back-pains, hip-pains, knee-pains, vertebrae out of alignment, the occasional migraine, etc.. Sometimes I was very lame and stiff. I remember on a bad night clutching at the banisters in order to get down the stairs without more pain than I could help.

There were a few positive things that happened in my life leading up to this time that are perhaps worthy of mention. One was that I had an enormous amount of pleasure with a beloved horse of my own, later referred to in this book as "Desert". I enjoyed both looking after him, as well as a certain amount of success in competitions. Of course I did not manage all of this without a considerable amount of help from other people. Part of this help came from visits to France's well known "Ecole d'Equitation Nationale", where riding with the "Cadre Noir" as it is best known, I learnt much about dressage that I did not know before.

My first visit in 1974 was the beginning of a big change in my attitude to learning foreign languages. All of the previous attempts to 'force' me to learn French had come at a time when I had no desire to travel, and was totally unmotivated, as I had considered it a complete waste of time and effort. I had convinced the people in my little world that I was totally incapable of learning it, until they had finally left me in peace. Ten years had passed since my academic education, and now I desperately wanted to understand what those French riding instructors were trying to teach me about horse riding. It seemed such an enormous task to tackle anything as vast as a whole language, but I decided that even a little would be an enormous breakthrough, so I tried. I went to night school, and also studied from teach-yourself French books when outside help was not available. I never achieved good French, but during this period of my life, and again in later years, I learnt enough to totally transform my trips abroad. This discovery, that other people's languages were well worthwhile struggling with, gave me the courage to tackle other tongues in later life, which enabled me to travel fairly freely, and gain experiences valuable for my spiritual life, which would have been hard to equal with English alone.

By living away from my family, I became to some extent independent, and started making arrangements for myself, which might never have happened if I had stayed at home. My mother had great difficulty trusting me to do anything, because of my apparent hopelessness with even the simplest things. I was inclined to see no point in making any special effort as long as someone else was there ready to do things for me. In many respects I had very caring parents. What I really craved was the kind of love that expressed itself in physical intimacy combined with the sort of love that goes hand in hand with openness, and closeness, and being and feeling understood by those around you, in this case, my parents. I was not capable of being open, and the physical intimacy that I longed for was rare and brief. So these things were largely missing, which made it seem easy for me to stay away from home as much as possible. When I was successful in life, I felt angry, because it showed me that I could do something well, and I felt that my talents had never been acknowledged at home, and especially not by my mother. If she did recognise my achievements, then I was incapable of knowing it. When I was unsuccessful, I always hid it if possible, because it caused me such pain if I thought that my parents knew about it. This was because their knowledge of any problems that I had caused them distress, and I could not bear to see that. Deep down inside me I loved them more than I knew, but I was growing increasingly secretive.

One of the things that had always helped me to keep my head above water during difficult times was my religion. I was brought up in the Church of England, and sent to a convent school, where the emphasis on religion was not surprisingly fairly strong. I became quite devout, and now had God and horses to run to in times of need. Usually in the various different places where I worked there would not only be a church, but also perhaps a choir to sing in, and a few friends maybe.

However, during this period of self imposed relative exile from my parents, I seemed to walk into more and more situations that I found very hard to cope with. Sometimes I felt very alone, and the day came when in spite of never having touched alcohol before, after someone had really let me down, I decided that I could not bear the intensity of my pain any longer, and that I would give alcohol a try. I was too well informed to believe that this could ever be a solution to my problems, but I thought that perhaps it could serve as a temporary measure to dull the emotional pain that I was living with until such time as I could find a better solution.

I climbed into my car, and drove myself to the nearest public house, where I bought myself a bottle of whisky. I chose whisky, because I thought that that was probably about the strongest, and would therefore be the most effective. That was the first time. It tasted horrible, but I managed to drink most of the bottle. (It was not a large one.) I became a secret drinker overnight. Looking back, I find it amazing how much whisky I managed to drink, and for how long, and mostly still manage my job, and with no one finding out. I think that was partly because I had most of it in the evenings, and I was definitely considered the least likely person on the premises to try any such thing. Finally, one evening I misjudged how much I could take and still manage to look after myself. I had to ask for assistance, and explain why I needed it. At first, before anyone came close enough to smell me, I was disbelieved, but then as I broke down in tears, it became all too obvious.

I expected that the woman I was telling would be furious with me, and I was afraid. (I was employed by her daughter at the time.) All that happened was, I experienced her love. It was real love. She realised that I drank because I was at my wits end, and knew not how to cope. She cared for me, and invited me to come and talk about things to her the following evening, when she was expecting me to be sober. I took a chance and shared with her, something that I have no memory of having risked before with anyone. Although she had no solution for me, her loving care had a very powerful effect. I was so moved by it, that I resolved that even if I did not stop my addiction, that this lady would never again have to bear the pain of helping me out, and I succeeded more or less.

My only slip was one night when although I was not drunk at the time, I fel so frustrated with everything that I started banging my head as hard as I could on the bathroom wall. Although it seems unlikely, the truth is that it had never entered my mind that someone might hear me, and wonder what was the matter. It was just another attempt on my part to cope with something that was just too much for me. While I was doing this, my previous rescuer knocked loudly on the locked bathroom door, so that I went and let her in, whereupon she asked me "What on Earth is the matter? Has my daughter upset you or something?" I could not tell her anything. I did not know myself. I was completely past knowing what could possibly be wrong with me. I just made a note that banging my head was a bad idea, because someone might hear me, and come along and start asking questions that I could not answer. Only years later did I learn during a psychology class at the local college, that sometimes children from deprived homes will bang their heads on the hospital walls in a frantic attempt to obtain some kind of stimulation. Where love is absent, pain is better than nothing, is what I learnt there.

I prevented anyone having to help me to bed after excessive alcohol again by making sure that I was already upstairs and in bed if need be before I became too helpless to manage it. I still hated the taste of whisky, in fact I could not find any form of alcohol that tasted good. Although I did manage through perseverance to partially acquire a slight liking for a few types of alcoholic drinks much later on, I meanwhile chose to force myself to swallow this foul tasting liquid in order to lose some of my awareness. When I was finding whisky too expensive, I would buy something cheaper. Sometimes I drank with other people, but mostly secretly. I found that if it was necessary, I could stop the habit any time.

Although part of me was trying to become an alcoholic, I could never reach this state of being unable to stop drinking that I had tried to attain. I could drink compulsively, and one glass was never enough. I drank at all times of the day, and during my worst spells, I would start my day with alcohol. My liver must have been doing a fantastic job, because I hardly ever had a bad head, although my thinking power was greatly reduced. I quite often lived on a combination of alcohol, large quantities of coffee, a lot of meat, and sometimes slimming pills as well. This made me very nervy, uneventempered, and gave me such a dreadful skin complexion that I frequently hated people seeing me, so I would stay out of sight when I could.

I was getting very disillusioned with the church at this time. There was a new parish priest, who always said that he was about to come round for a chat with me in the next few days. On the one hand, I did not like him, and although I politely replied, "Oh, how nice!", I found myself hoping that he would forget. When I realised after a few months that he would always forget, his insincerity began to annoy me. I also felt that the other church-goers were incapable of understanding that I was not always free to attend church, so I felt that they were critical, even if not openly. These things upset me, so I decided that whereas I had nothing against God, I did not like his church very much, so I stopped attending it.

Now I had no church in my life which left a gap. I kept away from my parents most of the time, and I had no close friends. I was always filled with the dread that if I spent too much time with any one person they would find out what I was like, and then there would be this rejection again. I was getting suicidal. Sometimes I would drink heavily, and then in an unfit state drive my car for miles. I was always half hoping that I might finish life with a fatal accident. The tricky part was how to do it so that I really did die, and not end up as an invalid for life, or injure someone else who would really have preferred to stay alive and intact. I considered alcohol, but somehow I found that too undignified. I could not see any point in continuing to live. I reasoned that my parents would not notice much difference, because I was so rarely at home anyway. I had no close friends to miss me, and nothing left on the Earth that I wanted to stay for except - - - my horse, "Desert." How could I ever be sure that if I left, another person would ever manage to love him enough? My love for this animal played a stronger part than anything else in keeping me on the Earth. I could almost say that I owed my life to him. Certainly, he made it easier for me to stay here, or harder to go, which ever way you prefer to look at it.

One evening I was pouring myself a drink, and wondering how hopelessly drunk I could manage to get myself that night, and how much damage I could do to myself. I was wondering how many brain cells I had so far managed to kill off, and if I was already past any chance of full repair, when I clearly heard a voice saying to me, "You had better look after that brain of yours. You might need it again some day." For a moment I put down the bottle in surprise. I was not accustomed to voices who spoke to me in an empty room. Yet it was a friendly voice, and I was unable to forget what it had said. Someone once asked me how and when did I come to have a sense of mission. At the time I could not recall when that had started, but I think that this moment was when the first inkling of it arrived.

It was at this point in my life in the Spring of 1979 that from this very low ebb, I began a steady rise. Interesting things started to happen to me. I began to get visions, and evidential dreams. It was sometimes like a stream of events or coincidences that gradually opened my eyes to truths about myself and life on Earth, and other places that I had simply never contemplated before.

My grandmother (my father's mother) and Winston Churchill seemed to be working together to raise me up out of my lethargic state, and to help me get started on my spiritual pathway. It helped me enormously that I had abandoned the Church, as I was left much more open minded without it, and felt much free-er to take up new beliefs.

Now for a little about these two helpers who approached me from a dimension on the other side of death, from their present reality. My grandmother's interest is perhaps not so very surprising. She had done what she could for me before she died, and with her love she came again to me then. Her first visit was in a dream. My spiritual waking up process was already beginning, and I was reading a book about spirit communication, in which there were a number of old English words that I did not know. Some of them I looked up in my dictionary, but when the word 'barter' came up, which I did not understand, it was at such an exciting point in the story, that I could not bear to stop reading for long enough to find out what it meant. That night in a dream, my grandmother came, and she brought with her a large dictionary. She opened it for me, and pointed to the definitions of 'barter'. Her dictionary was red, and 'barter' was written on the right hand side of the page. There were two definitions given, both of which I was able to read. She came dressed in a tweed skirt which was mostly pink, just like one that I had seen her wearing in life here.

The next morning I could clearly remember the dream, but thought nothing of it. That evening, however, I was really curious to find out what 'barter' actually meant. I opened my blue dictionary, and found 'barter' on the left hand side of the page. The meanings given were the same as those that I had been shown in my dream, but in reverse order. "How could someone who is dead come in a dream and give me valid information?", I wanted to know. "Is there perhaps some kind of life after death as we know it?" Of course the Church taught that there was life after death, but it had never been more than some vague theory in my head, rather like some kind of unlikely myth, where no one really knows if there could be any truth in it or not. Once the contact had been made with me, and I accepted that my grandmother still lived somewhere, she was able to approach me in my waking hours, which had the advantage that I did not have to try and remember dreams. In one instance, I had gone to a public house with a group of friends, and I was just swilling down my third glass of wine, when she advised me to leave the pub and go home. This involved offending the man who had brought me and wanted to drive me home himself about twenty minutes later. He was rather drunk and angry, but I would not stay. Instead I walked home late at night in the dark with a man who I had never met before with thoughts in the back of my mind of how horrified my mother would be if she knew what I was doing.

The following morning I noticed that my would-be chauffeur of the previous evening had a wound on his cheek. I found out that both he and those who left later with him had been attacked and robbed as they tried to leave the public house. Four of them had been knocked to the ground on their way to the car park. My grandmother had done her work thoroughly. Not only had she sent me home in safety, but perhaps in case I should have failed to listen to her, she also sent me without my passport, which I had hidden in my bedroom. (I was in Germany.) The preceding night when I went out, I had taken it with me, and also the following night. Only this time did I leave most of my money and my passport in my room.

Since these times, although she lives her own life in another place quite separately from me, I have periodically become aware of her presence in moments of need.

Winston Churchill also met me first in a dream. I found myself in the middle of London, and we walked the whole length of a street together in conversation. We were talking about the youth of today, mainly the ones who lack purpose and live destructive lives vandalising and breaking the law. Although I could not remember a word of this conversation afterwards, the content stayed with me, and also the amazement that I felt when I discovered that he and I could get on so well together, and that our views were so similar. If I had met someone so well known in the flesh, I would doubtless have been too shy and nervous to say anything.

When I recounted this amazing story to my mother, she was able to tell me exactly which part of London I was in. It was an area that I did not know, but my mother, who had lived in London for some time years ago, was able to tell me exactly where it was. That was the only part that was easy for her. "Why should Winston Churchill want to talk to a simple country-loving girl like you?", she exclaimed. I tried to tell her how I had recently learnt that 'spirits' sometimes try to help and guide people who are still living here in physical bodies on the Earth. "Even if they do, surely he is wasting his time with you? He ought to be talking to some belligerent communist instead", she went on. I made the point that maybe such a person would not be listening, and would not take any notice anyhow. My mother looked very worried, but fortunately restrained herself from telephoning the nearest lunatic asylum. However, I had noticed her expression, and decided not to push my luck too far in the future.

As I see things now, I find it hardly surprising that someone who had played such a crucial role in the history of the planet should still be interested in helping here today. I have since learnt that he was a Spiritualist in his last Earth incarnation, and so it is only natural that he should come not only to me, but to many others also. He has spoken directly to me quite a few times since that dream, and also through other mediums, at least two of which were rather surprised as they knew nothing of what had gone previously in my life. The third one had channelled him before, and that was for a whole group of people. I was wary of mentioning his name to people, and even of putting it in this book for fear that it might bring a reaction such as "Here we have a real little snob!", or "This one must think that she's really important!", etc.; but when we remember that many of us have played many different roles in our past lives, often ranging from king or queen to dustman or prostitute, good lives and bad lives as the great or the small, then I find that one cannot help starting to see the whole concept of social class and position quite differently. When I pass through death's door, I know that whatever life I have just been living is finished. I know that whatever and whoever I was, I am no more. It was just an identity.

I did not realise all of that at the time these things started, as I knew nothing then of reincarnation. Therefore I did feel rather in awe of this friendly presence who even said, "You can call me 'Winny' if you like." I thought this to be an unlikely name for him until I was guided to a book in which I saw on the page where I first opened it a copy of a letter from Winston to his mother. It ended "Your loving son, Winny."

Although I seldom channel for other people, I have sometimes been aware of his presence at such times. He told me that it was hard work trying to persuade me to pass on the concepts that I was being given to the people who I was channelling for. His part in this was to help me find the words with which to convey these feelings and ideas etc. that I was receiving telepathically. The messages were not his, but he was acting as a middle man. On one occasion the third person looked like an angel, whereas he was looking healthy, but somewhat overweight! "There is a fat man here telling me how to word all this," I explained to my friend. I knew that he was approving of my description, because I could feel his sense of humour.

You may be wondering why I needed so much help in order to understand psychic phenomena and the continuation of life after death if I had known psychic ability as a child. "Education" is the reason. I was taught to believe that the things I saw and felt were untrue; that is that they were merely part of a childish imagination. I remember my bitter disappointment when my mother told me that even fairies were not real. They were just make-believe things for children, but grown-ups knew better than to give any credence to such illusions. This information hit me like a stone. "Aren't angels real either?", I asked in upset tones. "Well yes, they do exist, but they are invisible." I found this difference hard to understand. Fairies, I had been told, were invisible also; so why could not they be real? Equally, if fairies were invisible and not real, then how could one be sure that the invisible angels were not also unreal? It was all very perplexing.

I also had been fascinated by the concept of witches, and delighted in painting them with their broom-sticks flying through the sky in our school art classes, aged ten or eleven. That was when we were not obliged to paint still life scenes of fresh fruit etc. However, when the art mistress saw what I had done, for once I was praised. "This child has a good imagination," she said.

So it seems that up until this time, I had spent my life not discovering my inner knowing, but unlearning it, in fact burying it thoroughly. Therefore starting in my early thirties was this slow but thorough relearning process. I began to get prognostic visions. They came spontaneously. I was never looking for them at the time. One of the most powerful came when I was sitting alone *in my lodgings mending a glove. I saw in full colour a scene with a* horse. I watched fascinated as someone led this animal up the ramp and into my horse lorry. The horse hesitated half-way up the ramp, but with a little persuasion agreed to go in. I saw the autumn colours on the trees and bushes there, and it was good weather. I recognised the horse, and I knew that I liked him, and also that I needed a new horse. It looked very much as though I was going to buy this one.

About six weeks later that Spring I met the owner, and asked tentatively if she knew of any horses for sale that might be suitable for me, but of course without mentioning my vision. She knew of none. "Oh dear!" I thought to myself, "My vision was just *an idle dream. I had better forget it, and try to live in the world of* reality." So I went off to look for another horse. What a tale of woe and sorrow and anxiety and frustration! Everything went wrong. I found myself dealing with a woman who seemed to be totally ruthless and unscrupulous. She tried to sell me a horse who turned out to be suffering from a permanent lameness for a large sum of money. To cut a long story short, I lost a lot of money, first in veterinary fees, and then even more in order to avoid a court case, where my solicitor advised me that I had little chance of winning in spite of my innocence. The would-be vendor ended up rich at my expense. Mercifully I managed to persuade her to keep the horse, but it was difficult. As soon as this miserable affair was over, I heard from the lady owning the horse which I had seen in my vision, asking me if I had found anything yet, as she would like to sell me hers. I bought hers. When I collected this lovely animal, it was Autumn. I stood back and watched as he was loaded into my lorry, and saw a perfect replay of my vision. He even hesitated on the way in, just as I had seen it six months previously.

I learnt a lot from this. If I had trusted my vision, I would never have had such a horrid time trying to keep myself out of court, and spending all that money in order to manage it. Secondly, it showed me that it was possible to move through time. I could not deny my own clairvoyance, even though I was unable to control it. Either I got a vision, or I did not.

The result of this and other happenings was that I was led by my intuition to become familiar with, and part of, two different spiritualist churches. I was very interested in learning more about all of these things. Here were people who took it all seriously. Furthermore, they were not only interested in spirit return and clairvoyance, but also in spiritual healing, otherwise known as the *laying on of hands*, just as Jesus taught it. I met some very loving and helpful healers, and experienced their healing first hand.

In September of 1981 I became redundant. Jobless meant nowhere to live, as accommodation went together with the job, so I had to make a move. I was really upset by all this. For one thing, I loved the man I had been working for, although I had never let him find that out. The relationship only existed on my side, and was consequently very distant. He had married someone else during the time that I was working for him, and I had been really careful not to do anything that might have upset his new wife. It was a painful relationship, but this enforced move away from him left me feeling heart-broken. I also minded losing the job, even though I knew deep inside myself that I was overdue for a change in order to grow as a person. During the period that followed, one of the biggest changes in my life was the sudden increase of free time, which I was able to use for studying psychic phenomena.

In 1982, I started buying my own food, and intuitively took a turn towards vegetarianism. With some kind of religious beliefs back in my life, I found the strength and motivation to almost eliminate alcohol from my diet. I began to realise that it was caffeine amongst other things that was irritating my skin, and causing me such a bad complexion. I noticed how after a caffeine drink, (usually three or four at a time in my case) my skin would start to feel hot, itchy and uncomfortable, so I gave up that as well. The result of all these changes was that a very old woman (I was not old, but especially on lame days, I felt very old.) began to grow younger again. I started to be able to manage long walks without pain, and I even lost some weight without the use of slimming pills. Encouraged by those around me, I started training to become a healer.

When I heard a story that the best healers are all vegetarian, and that they do not drink alcohol as it decreases their healing energy, I decided to live like that totally, instead of just 90%, with a consequent further improvement in my health. The suicide idea was definitely out of the question. I knew for certain that it could not end everything, because life after death had become a fact for me, not to mention having met someone who told me that if you commit suicide, you have to come back again.

I did not know then that most of us experience many lives on Planet Earth, and therefore this seemed a serious threat. Thinking that if I came back because I had committed suicide, then I would have to live another whole life, instead of just the rest of this one, was an alarming thought. After all, I could not be sure that I would not be born into a far worse situation next time, and find myself trying to endure three times the amount of suffering. It was definitely not worth the risk.

After much hesitation, I decided not to take another job, but to become a free-lance self-employed riding instructress. This necessitated finding my own house, as I would need my own telephone. Also I was very tired of living in places where the other people did not like or want me. I was determined to create a better reality for myself, and I did.

On 2nd. February, 1983 I moved into my own house. I found it wonderful to have a place that I could call my own. Of course it brought with it its share of problems, but on balance I found it a very good thing indeed, and I have lived there ever since.

From the security of my own home I started the free-lance work with horses. Sometimes I thought that I might prefer to give it all up, and do something else instead, but there were at least two snags. One was that I could not find an interesting alternative that I was capable of, and the second thing was that I still had a horse of my own (later in the book I have referred to him as "Wilderness"), and I simply could not bear to give him up. Once again it was a horse who was really determining my direction, and the key word was "love". So I have stayed with horses.

Another little incident that took place at about this time concerned my sense of mission again. At one of the meetings that I sometimes attended with the Spiritualist Church, a medium there revealed me she was 'being told' that I had come to the Earth with a mission to carry out. I had difficulty believing this, but the idea did appeal to me. I imagined that it would just be some small task, perhaps an afternoon's work one day, but I had no idea what it might be. Another time a friend and medium, who I had gone to visit for some tea, channelled for me that "For a soul as advanced as yours, there is more important work to do than looking after horses." It was followed by an acknowledgement of the good and noble qualities of the horse, so I knew that it was no slight on the animals.

Yet another time when I visited somebody's house, I met a man who told me that his gift was that when he looked at people, he could see their profession written across their foreheads in black letters. Now when he looked at me, he saw "Teacher" written not in black, but in gold. "Therefore", he said, "it must mean that you are a spiritual teacher". As far as I can remember, I told him that I did not have the knowledge to be one of those, but what he had said stuck in my memory, and gradually began to add to my sense of mission. All of these little signposts helped to arouse my curiosity in who I really was, and motivated me to travel further down the spiritual pathway in the hopes of finding out, and perhaps discovering some kind of purpose for being here in a body.

There was a Swiss friend of mine who lived in Germany who I liked to visit twice a year. She would help me with my riding, and we had esoteric interests in common. Sometimes I would channel for her a little. She encouraged me with this, and helped me to see what talents were developing in me. Her husband was also a help with this, as he had died just before I first met his wife. On one occasion, he appeared to me very clearly, and I was able to note waist upwards exactly what he was wearing. The picture remained with me so strongly, that when I was shown a video of him with some horses about six months later, I could recognise not only him, but also every garment that he was wearing. I had never seen those clothes before, not even in a picture. One Spring I telephoned my friend to ask if I could make my usual visit, and she told me with regret, that she was about to spend some considerable time in the United States, so she would not be able to have me. However, she made a suggestion. She thought that I should go to Austria, where a friend called Linda Tellington-Jones was leading a week-long clinic with horses. She told me that she was sure that it would be a great help to me. This kind lady sent me information through the post, and I applied for a place on Linda's clinic to be held near Saalfelden in Austria. I was feeling rather half-hearted about the whole thing at the time. I supposed that we would ride quite a bit, which can only mean that I had not really studied the details properly.

Linda's work is unusual, and very fine. What she teaches are not just techniques to make animals do or be things, but a means of man-animal communication that is of enormous benefit to both on many levels. It contains many inbuilt healing properties. I really was not ready to become fully involved with all this, but I became strongly addicted to the fascinating evening discussions that took place amongst a select few of us. I had my first glimpse of tarot cards, and I discovered that Linda believed in re-incarnation, and that she had obviously been regressed quite a few times herself. I had recently taken considerable interest in this, but had heard so many tales about the dangers involved in this type of hypnosis, that I had not the courage to go to anyone to experience it. I looked carefully at Linda, and thought to myself, "This lady has been regressed perhaps many times, and yet I am quite sure that she is perfectly all right. Therefore, perhaps if I went to the same therapist that she has used, then I would still be all right afterwards as well." So I asked Linda's advice, and she gave me the name of "Rhea Powers" written on a small slip of paper along with two telephone numbers so that I could get in touch. After I arrived home, I managed to lose this little slip of paper immediately, so I had to abandon that plan, and this was at the end of March.

Life at home carried on much the same as usual with the horses. I was not particularly happy. I suffered from depression quite a lot, but then I had done that for a large part of my life, and I considered it a normal way for me to be. Sometimes I would ponder on whether or not it was actually possible to become "undepressed", but having no idea how to change things, I simply carried on how I was. Looking back, I can see that there were small signs that my parents were not sure if I was really happy or not, but there was nothing that they could have done at this stage, especially as I never admitted that I had any problems. (Actually, there had been two exceptions to this. The first was when I was trying to avoid buying the lame horse a few years back, and the second was when I decided to purchase my own house. On both occasions, I both asked for and took advice from my father, who was very helpful.)

There is one particularly interesting realisation that has come to me since I have been putting this story together, and that is that I really did have two parents who cared about me. Before that, I was already very clear about the problems that I had had with them, especially when it came to trying to cope with my mother's inability to relinquish her grasp and feelings of responsibility for me, that made it so hard for me to become myself if she was anywhere around, and had made it particularly difficult to adopt my own belief system, as she clearly felt that my religious beliefs were still her responsibility, and not mine. I also knew about the resentment I felt, because she seemed far more interested in getting someone else to look after us when we were children, than doing it herself. (In some ways this was a blessing, because I found her very impatient, and her quickness and punctuality did not go at all well together with my slow dreaminess and lateness. She said to me years later, "But you were so slow at everything, and you never wanted to go anywhere with us, because you were always afraid that you were going to miss a ride on your pony." Every word of that was true.) Also my sister and I had fought each other constantly, which led her to openly admit to us how thankful she was each time we returned to our boarding school. Yet another system for getting us out of the way, I felt.

When I was twenty-three, she managed to hurt me more than at any other time that I can remember. She told me that I was now much too old to go on kissing her. All that I had ever tried to do for years was to give her a quick one on the cheek at bed time. She had trained me to do it quickly, and not to touch her anywhere with my hands at the same time. Also I must not hover round her like a moth waiting my chance to do it. I must get on with it quickly. Now even this treasured privilege was taken away from me. "How could a mother be so unloving, and so unappreciative of affection?" I asked myself. As I had long ago learnt to do, I suppressed my grief, and carried on as though nothing had happened. I even succeeded in hiding it from myself just how deeply I had been hurt.

Only years later when hopelessly drunk did this incident surface again, and in the mist of my tears, to my own amazement, I found myself telling someone how much she had hurt me. Long afterwards I was to realise that it was not all kisses that were banned, but only kissing good night. A kiss after long periods away from home was still allowed. Even that discovery did not heal very much, because it seemed so awful, that I was only adequately lovable for affection from me to be acceptable, if I first stayed away from her for long enough.

There are two sides to every coin, and I expect that the other side of this one is covered with tales of how I hurt my mother, or made her angry through my thoughtlessness etc.. For example, I learnt far more recently that my tendency to giggle when I wanted to kiss her was disliked, although I have lost any memory of that myself.

It seems to be a very popular New Age thing to uncover all of these parental problems, and sort them out; but nothing that I have ever done has made me aware of how much, or whether or not they actually loved me before I started writing this book. It has made me see how especially in my early life, my parents were constantly concerned about my welfare. It can't have been easy sending a child like me to school, knowing that I was going to hate every minute of it. Then they paid a lot of money for my education, while I for my part did my best to avoid learning everything if I could, and was not grateful for any of it. After all, I would have chosen everything quite differently for myself if I had had a choice. My mother was only occasionally what I wanted her to be, but I was unable to see that even when I hated what she did, or she made mistakes with me, which she undoubtedly did, as most mothers do, that she actually had done the best that she knew, and mostly with very few thanks from me.

So back to the story. The weeks passed, and brought the summer with them. One summer afternoon I was tidying out the cupboards in my study where I do all my paper work, when a tiny little slip of paper fell out of something. I picked it up from the floor, and saw that it had the name of "Rhea Powers" on it with the two telephone numbers, one for the States, and the other was a contact number for her in London. I sat down on the floor, and looked at it thoughtfully. Several times recently in my meditation I had seen the letters 'R P', and wondered what they meant. Suddenly it was clear. They stood for Rhea Powers, and now must be the time for me to follow this up. I tried the London number, only to discover that the person to contact had moved. Luckily the new occupier was able to give me the new number. I tried that, but could not find the person at home. Finally someone who was there gave me a day time work number to try. Still no luck, but a message got through, and at last, someone who knew about Rhea called me back. It turned out that I was enquiring at exactly the right time to book myself a private session with Rhea in July. There were only two possibilities left, and fortunately 9th. July

1985 was suitable for me. It was to take place in someone's London flat. I was very nervous about it. Normally, if I needed to go to London, I would take the car, but not this time. I thought "Supposing that I get stuck in trance, or my etheric body gets trapped somewhere outside the rest of me? Maybe I won't know who I am any more afterwards, that I won't remember my way home, or where home is, or what I am supposed to do tomorrow." I had heard such dreadful tales of this "dangerous" therapy. Also I am a nervous type of person even in a safe situation.

So, on the appointed day, (having carefully written down in my diary who I was, where I lived, etc. just in case I forgot, and put the diary into my handbag,) I took a train which I estimated would get me to London with lots of time in hand. It did, but then after a light meal, it was still necessary to cross the city, and find the flat with Rhea in it. I would have arrived three-quarters of an hour early, if only things had gone how I had planned them, but they did not. It took me three trains instead of one. I started by boarding the wrong train, and setting off in the wrong direction. When I noticed this, I tried to correct my error by changing trains. Things seemed to be running more smoothly for a while, but in my panic, I got off the train too early, and when I came up from the London Underground into the street, I found myself in the wrong place altogether. So back down I went, queued to buy another train ticket, waited until another train came in, and this time I managed to stay on it long enough to reach my destination. I had been given clear directions on the telephone about how to find the flat, but although it was all beautifully written down in my diary, I had forgotten that it was a flat, and was looking for the wrong number on one of the street doors. Not surprisingly, I could not find it, so I started looking somewhere else for it instead. Still no luck, so I started walking back down the street.

As I hesitated outside what was actually the right door, a young man turned up, and noticing my lost expression, asked if he could help. Rescued at last, he escorted me up the stairs to the flat where Rhea was waiting for me. My late arrival did not please her, for she was working extremely hard to a very tight schedule. It got worse when I asked to go to the bathroom. Nerves do dreadful things to you, and in addition to everything else, I had sweated so badly from sheer fright, that I needed to wash and change my blouse before I considered that I was fit to go near anybody. When I eventually re-emerged from the bathroom, there was only just over an hour left of my hour and a half appointment. I thought that it was just bad luck that had made me so late, but my philosophy having changed since then, I can now see that due to extreme fear, my subconscious had organised a few delays for me in order to shorten the session.

Once started, it went pretty smoothly, and none of the things that I had feared took place. As Linda had told me, "You will be perfectly safe with Rhea, she's super!" You may wonder why on earth I did it if I was so afraid. Well, it is part of my character to dare myself to do things that frighten me; a little bit in order to prove to myself that I am not such a coward as I believe I am! In this instance, there were deeper motivating factors, primarily that I was engrossed in my personal research of all of the unseen realities that I could discover. I went to this regression not in order to find out what I had done or been, but to discover whether or not I had had a past life, and if so was it possible to remember it. I was to some extent sceptical, but really keen to find out.

In spite of having missed the first part of my session, it turned out to have an extremely powerful working in my life. "This woman has changed me more in less than an hour and a half, than anyone else has ever done in years!", I thought to myself, and I began to be filled with feelings of deep gratitude. This was really a step forward, and I wanted to take another, or maybe many more of them.

Unfortunately, Rhea did not come to work in London again, so two years later I was still waiting for her. One night I had a dream, in which I was searching for her in central London. I found a large building, and inside were six therapists, two men, and four women. I asked them if they knew where Rhea Powers was. They answered, "But we could help you as she is not here." I looked round at them, and I could see that two of them might be suitable for me, but I wanted Rhea. "Wait until September", one of them said, and I left. This dream stayed in my mind from April when it came until September, by which time I had still heard nothing of her, and the contact in London could not help. On about 29th. September, when I had lost all hope, someone with whom I was sharing a room during a "Healing" workshop at the Findhorn Foundation in Scotland, happened to say casually to me, "... and then there is Rhea Powers of course." I had not mentioned her, but here was someone who not only knew her name, but was also able to put me back in touch with her, and give me her new address in Germany. This was as promised in my dream. Although not how I thought it would be, my ray of hope had duly arrived in September. My informer, Giselheid McKenzie, was to help me again later in my life, as you will read when I come to that time.

All this resulted in my going to Hamburg, Germany to participate in the "Light Worker Training" lead by Rhea and Gawain Bantle, to whom she is now married. By this time, she was working rather differently, but somehow I felt that my guardian angels or my higher self was guiding me to participate. The guidance was good, and I felt that it did much to help develop my psychic awareness and ability. Also I felt a much free-er and happier person.

The transformation was not complete, but it was considerable. It caused some subtle change, which gave me a strong desire to reconnect with Linda Tellington-Jones. Gawain was able to give me the telephone number of someone who might know where she was. I was in luck, and at the end of November the same year, I was able to join one of Linda's trainings near Hamburg.

There is something about being with or talking to Linda that seems to work like a catalyst in me. All sorts of things start to happen. This time it triggered a real landmark in my life: the beginning of the animal channellings that have caused me to write this book, and which began quite soon afterwards. I found myself filled with them, but had no one in whom I dare confide. Eventually I decided that this was simply too much to go on carrying around inside me, so I decided to try the only person that I knew who was not likely to advise medical assistance. That was Linda. I had never tried to telephone anyone who lived so far away before, and I was really concerned that she would not be interested in staying on the line long enough to for me to relate my unimportant little story, but I had to speak.

It is not always easy getting Linda on the telephone. Much of her time is spent away from home, and when she is there, she is often very busy. On top of this, there are seven or eight hours of time difference between New Mexico and England. I kept on trying, and on my fifth or sixth attempt, instead of her assistant or the answering machine, I finally reached Linda rather late one evening (British time). I began somewhat apologetically to recount my first animal stories to her. I was at least a third of the way through, and she was still listening patiently. "Can it really go on like this?", I asked myself. "Will this busy lady really stay on the line long enough for me to tell all?" To my amazement, Linda was still there as I reached the end of it, and when I stopped, to my even greater amazement, I discovered that she was not just putting up with me as a favour, but was really interested. Could I please write some of this down for her? She knew some people who she felt really ought to hear it. I agreed, provided that she kept my identity secret. I was still very afraid of anyone other than her finding out what I was doing or experiencing. Part of me was longing to share it all with the world, but even though Linda, who works more closely with animals than anyone I know, learnt from them that I was not being given the information in order to keep it secret, but to share it, I still attached a disproportionately high level of importance to the opinions, approval and acceptance of me by other people. I feared disbelief and ridicule both regarding the channelling and myself. These difficulties were largely overcome by my sessions with the Light Institute, some of which are described later in the book.

Really I was overjoyed. Ever since the first inkling that I came to Earth for a specific purpose dawned upon my consciousness, I had been searching for it. Now that it was apparent to me that I was not on the earth-plane by some unfortunate accident, but through conscious intent, no matter how many misgivings I might have about it; I knew that the greatest hurt and disappointment that I could possibly inflict on myself would be to die without having discovered and fulfilled my purpose and mission allotted for this specific lifetime. This was the only way the suffering that I had so far endured could possibly be justified. Of course there are other things that I desire from life such as fun and games, and lots of horses, and travel, and excitement, and so on; but to do that for which I came is my number one goal. I have never had any lasting joy in carrying out tasks that I felt could be just as easily accomplished by someone else. I have always, when there has been choice, tried to pick things for which I felt I was really needed. Maybe this animal channelling was only a very small beginning, but it really felt like my work, no matter how many other people may be working at something similar in other parts of the world.

Chapter 1
The Beginning

ne dull afternoon in early January of 1989 found me curled up in my favourite chair reading one of Linda's TTEAM Newsletters. (It has all sorts of interesting things in it about Linda Tellington-Jones's work, such as what is going on, and other people's experiences with case histories, etc.) In the 1988 April issue Linda describes just very briefly what she calls the "Council of Animals." She explains how she has received messages from them, not in dreams, but in broad daylight; and how other people who are willing to listen can do the same. She knew of at least one other couple who had.

Visualisation had always been fairly easy for me, so as I paused in my reading to take in this interesting information, I started to picture the animals sitting in a circle. However, it was not necessary to think of each one in turn, as the moment that I had the desire to do this, they were all instantly there. I was sitting in the centre of their circle, and the whole thing was situated in a grassy clearing in a wood. I did not need to think of that either, it was simply there. In spite of that, I was still under the impression that I was just playing games with my imagination. Nonetheless, I began to feel uneasy about it. I was often afraid of people, and now I was starting to wonder which I found the most alarming, being in the centre of a circle of people, or a circle of animals?

I was on the verge of thinking that it was people, but had not quite decided, when a voice said "You have almost got over your fear of people. You are nearly ready to work with us". This really gave me a shock. I could no longer suppose that I was just imagining things, because I knew for certain that I had not written the script! The voice seemed to come from somewhere near the giraffe. I looked round the circle, and could see that every animal represented a different species. They all seemed to be there, even a little grey rabbit sitting beside some blue hairbells. I had thought that I was more or less at ease with animals, so why did I find this such a challenge I wondered? Perhaps it was because I knew so little about them. Horses had filled my life so completely, that I had never tried to study any other kind of animal in depth. Some of these who were appearing before me are dangerous to man when they are in the physical dimension, and others I could not identify. Yet it was obvious to me that they could read all of my thoughts, and probably understood me even better than I did myself. That was my first encounter.

Having made the initial link with me, the ground had been prepared for further communication. So a few days later on 9th. January, it happened again. It was late evening, and I was sitting on the floor where I like to meditate before going to bed. As usual, I decided to spend a minute or two first choosing the best type of meditation for that particular night. While I was thinking about it, I noticed that the circle of animals had formed around me again. This time I was not afraid, as I remembered that lions or not, they were all on another dimension, and in no way a danger to me. Also, I was feeling their vibrations much more clearly now, and I knew that I loved them, and that their coming was very special to me. I felt that they were very special animals, and was rather overwhelmed that they thought it worthwhile to visit me. The mere fact that they came touched me very deeply. This is what followed.

First of all I saw the TTouch sign. This is like two capital Ts drawn together, TT. (I need to explain here, that this is something from Linda Tellington-Jones's work, and refers to the way in which touch is used mostly in circles on animals to help the animals in many different ways; for example, with their body awareness, relief from pain and fear, etc. Humans can benefit as well.) It was only the two Ts that I was shown. They appeared in shining gold very close to me just in front of my eyes. The top of them was decorated with poppy flowers and green leaves. The picture seemed to linger there for quite a while, so it was clearly intended that I remember it. After that went, I found myself focussing on the circle of animals again. I saw a ring of golden light, which seemed to run straight through the bodies of each of the animals linking them together as they sat in their circle. I wondered what this meant. "The magic circle", they said. I did not fully understand, but they kept on repeating, "The magic circle", again and again. Perhaps they were trying to emphasise and draw my attention to a truth already to some extent known. Circles and rings are extremely powerful. Much strength is inherent. It feels to me that this was a reminder. So ended my second encounter.

The following evening, I was meditating again. This time I was consciously carrying out a 'healing the planet meditation'. As taught in one of the spiritual workshops that I had recently attended, I was reaching out with my non-physical hands to lift Planet Earth up into the light. After a minute or two, I perceived other human hands working in the same fashion coming from other directions, who were also lifting the planet up. This phenomenon was something that had happened before, and so it did not surprise me in the least. The next events did!

I suddenly noticed that there was a beautiful leopard looking for his chance to help. Then I saw other animals gathering around. They all wanted to help. By now I was not receiving information entirely in words, but some as telepathic impressions. They showed me the power that human beings held, and how the vast majority of us had turned away from nature. They showed me this in pictures, and I could see that the path of mankind looked like a 'U' turn. Something else had caught my eye. It was the birds arriving, and then a magnificent tree surrounded by light. The trees were helping as well. I could see that man had badly interfered with the harmonious functioning of the planet. I could not help wondering why things had got so bad. If I were to ask myself that question, then I would suggest that it is all part of a learning process; but now is the time to learn how to turn round and put the damage right, which could be the most valuable lesson of all for us.

As I sat there looking at the representatives from the various different kingdoms, I heard the words "We are waiting! We are waiting!" repeated time and time again. They are waiting for us to turn around and work with them, and recognise that we are all part of the same consciousness, instead of carrying on as though man was the only form of life with a true value, and behaving with such a callous disrespect for most of the rest of creation. Of all the things that I saw that evening, the most impressive was the tree surrounded in light, which is why I now wish to go back in time a bit, and start to tell some of my experiences with trees.

Chapter 2

Trees

he beginning of interesting tree experiences started for me in this particular lifetime on 9th. October, 1988. I was attending meditation classes held in someone's private house, which were led by George Pratt, who I would describe as a trance medium, healer, and spiritual teacher. This particular night we were having a led meditation, and George asked us to look at an oak tree. (Visualise one.) No doubt we were given more directions than that, but this is the last one that I remember before I was drawn away into my personal experiences, regardless of anything that George may have been saying. We were a small group of people, and no doubt each one of us had a different story to tell afterwards. This was mine.

"I felt drawn towards this oak tree, and as I approached it, a very small door opened in its trunk, just like an invitation to enter. I looked inside, and saw a sort of dark brown density. I was hesitant to enter, as I was anxious not to hurt the tree. Then a very small man dressed in leaf green, and wearing a pointed hat, took my hand indicating that it was all right. We entered together. The door closed itself behind me, and I was no more aware of the little man in green. As my being took its place inside the tree, my arms and head stretched upwards becoming branches and foliage, whilst below the hips, I sank downwards stretching out into a complex network of roots in the good soil of Mother Earth. I was aware of the soil particles from which I could draw nourishment, and the molecules of oxygen and moisture lying in between the soil particles, and lying against my root fibres. I felt my roots gradually expanding, as their network crept through the earth. I felt the flexibility of my trunk, and the courser lined texture of the bark around it as I swayed to and fro in the wind, with my branches reaching upwards to the sky capable of withstanding even greater movement.

I saw Autumn come, and my leaves fall. As they fell, my being released them, and I felt no pain. It was all a natural part of nature's rhythm, which left my being intact. I saw myself standing alone on a green hill. A man was approaching with an axe on his shoulder. There was no communication between us. He walked up to me, and without a word as though I were some dumb unfeeling object with no right to life on the planet, he cut me down. There was no explanation given; no permission asked. I was helpless against the power of his axe. I saw his little house appear on the hillside, built partly with my wood. I looked at the base of my trunk, now open to the sky. The sap was still oozing upwards out of it, but gave life to no tree, for I had been cut away. For a while this bare stump bled sap into the atmosphere, unable to reach the branches. I was suffering from acute shock. My feelings were numbed, as my spirit slowly drifted away from that place.

I had known only life and harmony, and felt connected to other life until the man had arrived."

Well, what happened to me there, I wonder? There are various possibilities. One is that I really had known life as a tree on this planet. That it was one of my incarnations. Another is that I was allowed to experience this on another dimension only in 1988 in order to understand how the trees feel. All this is only valid thinking if one accepts linear time as the only reality. If one dismisses that, which means that everything happens simultaneously anyhow, then it does not make a great deal of difference. It means that I was, am, will be the tree or not.

There are many ways of seeing it. Which one of them is the most acceptable is of little importance to me. What really counted was that I received insights that I could never have gained by any other way that I know of, and that I can pass them on to others with open ears, so that this total insensitivity so often shown by mankind towards the plant kingdom can be reduced. Clearly, if one must cut a tree down, one should communicate with the spirit of the tree first, and reach an agreement about it. This would base the action on mutual co-operation with the plant kingdom.

Following these experiences, I went to spend Christmas with my mother as usual. Also as usual, I took myself for a walk on December 26th. in the woods near her home. It is seldom that I am walking anywhere without being in a hurry, but as I had more time than usual, I was really keen to find out if I could make use of a little tree communication that I had read about in one of Linda's news letters. I picked out a tree that I felt attracted to, and went over to it. Before I had time to start what I had in mind, the tree spoke. "All is not good here. Many things are wrong." I could feel the distress of the tree in my body, and how the tree was trying to raise the alarm, and be heard, for it was in the interests of the planet, but most of us pass by without giving it a thought, and with deaf ears. Now I was ready to start.

It is known as the "Flowering Tree Ceremony", and was taught to Linda by Rupert Sheldrake, one of the World's leading-edge scientists. You start with your back to the south side of the tree, and ask the question "Who am I?". Then you move to the north side and ask "Where do I come from?". Next on the west side ask "What am I doing here?". Finally on the east side ask "Where am I going?".

So it went like this:

"Who am I?"	Helena.
"Where did I come from?"	A sacred place.
"What am I doing here?"	Learning.
"Where am I going?"	To a sacred place. Upwards, like me.

The last three words seem to have been added as an afterthought, probably because I was feeling dissatisfied with the brevity of the replies. It is interesting to note, that if you practise this, gradually the answers seem to get longer, and much more explicit. However, I did not know that at the time, and assumed that this was typical. Also I can see now that I was most likely blocking a lot of the information myself, as I had the thought in the back of my mind that "A tree is unlikely to know anything about me, and if it does, then I doubt that I can hear it".

I took my leave of the tree, being in some haste by now. (My mother was sure to be wondering why I was still outside in the dark, for dusk had already arrived.) As I walked away, I found that I was still in communication with the spirit of the tree. Again I saw it open itself to me, and from the heart of it stepped out a nature spirit, manifesting as a tiny little man in green with a pointed red hat. He was only a little taller than my knees. We greeted one another with a sensation of mutual joy and wonder. I felt myself slide my hand over his shoulder and down his back as we met, and he reached out to touch my arm on the other side. It was a lovely energy that flowed between us. I felt surprise and pleasure on both sides. He told me how much it meant to him to have this contact with human consciousness. It felt as though a door had been opened between the two worlds, and that sadly and wrongly, it is usually closed. It is in our power to open it.

Having now written about the greater part of my previous contact with trees, I am now moving on to the 18th. January, eight days after my vision of the tree surrounded in light, which had represented the tree consciousness playing its part in giving healing to the planet. I was still of the opinion that trees were rather basic things, and therefore not ideal for channelling information. To me they were part of the lower realms of nature.

As I began to meditate, I saw a beautiful pine tree. Then other representatives of the tree kingdom began to arrive, until there were many of them. Slowly and painstakingly, they started to tell me more of their inner nature than I had ever previously been aware of. It was clear to them that I regarded them as a second or third rate channelling medium for wisdom and knowledge. "Look at us!", they cried. "Can you not see how without exception we have manifested the God-power within us as well as has been possible in the many varied conditions where we have grown? Never have we violated the laws of the Universe. We continue always to be as perfect as it is possible for us to be, serving the

Earth in every way that we can. If our existence on the Earth is so untainted, if we have always expressed the God-force which governs us just as we were intended to, why do you consider us such an inferior channel for light?"

This did change a few things for me! I felt very humble before these magnificent beings now. I saw how erroneous my former judgement of them had been. I thought now of the previous wrong-doings of mankind, and realised how relatively hard it is for us 'tainted' ones to become pure channels for wisdom and light.

Chapter 3

A Question of Identity

he following day, far from sitting in a suitable and 'correct' position for meditation with a straight spine, I was comfortably curled up in an armchair reading a book. After all, I was reading, not meditating. Nonetheless, I put my book down in order to think about the circle of animals who had visited me before. Thinking about them turned out to be enough to bring them along.

Previously I had been filled with wonder that they came. This time, after my experience with the trees, I realised that it was not enough to feel touched that they bothered to come, but I must regard them as equals; that I must love and respect them as fellow dwellers of the Universe who ran on the same God-energy as I did. The animals felt this change in me. They responded by coming closer, and allowing a cautious but mutual exchange of love. I watched the first one to approach me, wishing to identify it. As I explained before, my knowledge of animals other than horses was very poor. I thought that this particular animal might be some kind of leopard, as I studied the markings on its coat. "I'm a tiger," it said. "You can't be!" I replied. "Your coat is not right for that." It gave up trying to convince me, and allowed me to stroke its beautiful back. When I am communicating with other beings in this way, I find that I am mobile quite independently of my physical body.

My consciousness can move around either with or without a body, and freely interact with whatever, or whomever I am relating to at the time. Sometimes I consciously control it, and other times it seems to live a life of its own, especially in my deeper meditative states. So when I say that I was stroking the back of this animal, my physical hand was most probably perfectly still. When the animals all seemed to be very close to me, I started to wonder what we could do next. They had read my thoughts as usual. "We will show you," they said. Immediately there appeared two trees before me. They stood with their trunks like pillars, one on either side of the beginning of a path that I must follow. As I started along this pathway through the forest, I was aware of many different animals on all sides of me. I followed the path, while they walked through the trees on either side of it, visible in all directions. I was surrounded by them. We all had the same destination. There was total silence, yet we were linked together in a common purpose. I kept looking at the elephant, not so far away on my right. He walked so majestically. He never turned his head to look at me. He was intent on where he was going, but I felt sure that he knew exactly where I was. The animal who claimed to be a tiger walked close by me on the other side, and loved it when I touched him.

After a while, I broke the silence by asking them where we were going. I was then shown how the path sloped gently upwards, and how the stream that we passed was becoming clearer and cleaner, the impurities draining out of it, and ahead was a beautiful place filled with a soft golden light. I understood that the light was home, the presence of God, the Source, or however you like to describe it. The Light from which we came, and to which we all return eventually.

At this point my consciousness returned to normal. I left the armchair, and went to pick up a newspaper that had only just been pushed through my door by the newspaper boy. The first picture that I saw as I took it into the kitchen was of a tiger. It was exactly like the animal who said it was a tiger in my visions. I had no idea that tigers were so asymmetrically marked. I thought that they had perfectly matching stripes all over like most of the toy tigers that I could remember. How on earth could I have thought that I knew better than the tiger himself what kind of animal he was? Two days later I eagerly watched a television programme on tigers in some part of India. I saw how the coat markings varied, and many were very similar to those of my discarnate friend. Shortly after that while I was meditating, the tiger came to see me. This time, he was apparently on his own. I asked him if he would clarify the significance of the stream that I had been shown. I understood from him that it represented a cleansing of Creation on its way into the Light.

This had been a useful lesson in trust. Even though I had not shown any, it was a teaching that I could benefit from in more difficult cases, like the following case of identity.

I was attending one of George Pratt's meditation classes again. We had nearly finished, when I suddenly became aware of a small green entity waiting for his/her/its chance to communicate with me. As I never discovered what the sex was, I think that I will call it "him". I saw him slightly to my left, and turned my inner eye in that direction in order to take a closer look. There was certainly nothing human about this being, although one part did seem to be the head, and I know that I was being looked at. He was pale leaf-green, and as he appeared to me, his body appeared translucent. I wondered if this was an extra-terrestrial, for I know that they exist in many forms. "Yes, I am an extra-terrestrial," he replied to my unspoken question. "What do you do?" I asked. "I come here to help work on the molecules in the Earth's atmosphere, and to help clean it up." I thought that it was wonderful that this little light being was helping us, and I reacted by sending him thoughts of love. His little green form filled with a soft golden light, and we parted.

Afterwards I began to doubt, and wondered if maybe he was some kind of nature spirit of the air. Then I recalled that when he told me what he was, although he may have read my thoughts, I had never actually asked him that question, and therefore I was not expecting an answer just then, so I was surprised when I heard it, and that is how I reasoned that I had not thought it up for myself. Secondly, I remembered the lesson from the tiger, and consequently I decided to trust both of them.

The more communications that I receive, the clearer it becomes that I am being taught through them. It is not just the information that I am being given that teaches, but there are these inbuilt lessons about receiving and trusting. Perhaps I could call them lessons in mediumship, or channelling lessons. Certainly everyone of them that I have ever had has come in a perfect order. Many times when I have been given difficult information that was really hard to believe, or I was asking myself "Have I really got this right?" then there has been some other form of verification given to me. For example, the picture of the tiger in the paper, and many times it has been some other psychic saying "Oh yes, that is exactly what I was getting." So much of this seems to involve trust and confidence. I started out with very little of either, but I think that I am very slowly growing some.

"Ahead was a beautiful place filled with a soft golden light"

Chapter 4

Energy Vortices or Power Points

hilst sitting curled up in an easy chair with a book on my lap at home, I perceived what I took to be a leopard not far away from me. He clearly wanted my attention for some kind of communication. I said straight away that I had far too much on my mind to cope with anything of that nature at the moment, and especially not something that might need writing down afterwards. (Actually I have often found myself trying to consciously cut myself off from would-be communicators when I am feeling stressed. Even though I feel uneasy about that, I have always believed that if it is really important, then they will reach me somehow sooner or later. They always seem to. Sometimes it will happen in the smallest room of my house, just when I least expect to be spoken to!) In this instance, I asked the leopard if he would please wait for a day or two while I got the rest of my life into some sort of order, and then return, as I would be willing to help then. He looked disappointed, and then walked away.

By 27th. February, a few days later, my house and everything else in my environment was more or less in order. I felt tired, but I had peace of mind, and felt ready to listen. I meditated before going to bed as I often do. Having sat crossed-legged on the floor for a while, I lay myself down flat out on the soft carpet for a rest. I believed my meditation to be complete, and planned going up to bed in a minute or two.

While lying there, I became aware that there were two animals in the room with me, a lion and a leopard. I have already explained that when in this meditative state, I am keenly aware of a non-physical body in which I can freely relate to other things existing in a non-physical dimension. This occasion was no exception to that. This was one of the times when I was not really in control of the setting. The nonphysical body was lying on the floor in the same space as the physical one, the main difference being that it was not wearing any clothes. This would normally not have worried me, had it not been for the approach of two large 'wild' animals, which made me feel very vulnerable. I quickly reminded myself that they would not require meals of flesh in their present dimension, and tried to stay relaxed. I suppose that this was another lesson in trust for me.

On reaching my prostrate form, they started to nuzzle it, and I got the feeling that they wanted me to sit up and concentrate harder for them. So I sat physical and other bodies up together, and looked around. There was the circle of animals again, with one representative of each species as before. I saw again the ring of white light that connected them all together. I had the leopard snuggled up against my left side, and felt the lion's body against my right side. They felt very loving, and by now I was enjoying having them so close. We were all sitting in the same circle together. Then the giraffe, looking very tall and prominent, stepped forward as their spokesman. "We want you to speak for us," he said. I intervened very quickly to explain that I did not think that I was a clear enough or good enough channel to do the job right now, although I would like to help them when I became fit. Undaunted, the giraffe continued.

"We live on this planet as well. Our welfare is threatened. We would like a better understanding from mankind, a better relationship between us." The next bit was not nearly so easy for me to follow. He spoke of certain "pressure" points which exist in many different places on the earth, and said that these were very important. We should pay attention to these. I sat there wishing that I knew what was meant by pressure points, and why they were considered important, but no more information was forthcoming that night. Finally nobody spoke, and I looked round, and observed the most beautiful silence in the room, before we went our separate ways.

The following evening in one of George Pratt's classes, I saw the leopard not far away rolling about on the floor at the beginning of our meditation. As we finished meditating, I spotted the lion sitting very close to me, almost touching. Between them they managed to persuade me to start talking to George's meditation group about the animal channellings. It was really George's question time, and I had merely started talking with the intent of asking two small questions. Before I could stop myself, I found myself recounting the tale of the previous evening. When I had finished, I asked the animals "How did that happen?" "You agreed to speak for us," came the reply. So I had, I thought to myself, but I was not expecting to do it just now. This little incident made me start to realise that I was involved in something much bigger than me over which I had little control, and that although I would always be free to resist it, it seemed to be a commitment that had been made deep down at soul level.

Not long after these events, I began to get an intuitive feeling that the pressure points referred to might be openings at various places on the Earth, where the animals try to make their collective consciousness heard by us in this dimension. I later had evidence that this was so when I was visiting Arizona, but I will say more about that in detail when I get that far. It does, however, seem appropriate to skip forward in time to July of 1990, when I was in the Canary Islands visiting Lanzerote for a workshop run by Rhea Powers and Gawain. One afternoon we were climbing a steep hill, and when I reached the top of it, I decided to sit down in the sun, and try to tune in to the energies of the island. The first thing that I saw was two elephants, who told me that this was one of the pressure points that the giraffe had referred to. As this was an energy vortex, a phenomena also referred to as a power point, I now knew what was meant. It is well known among psychics that power points are not all the same, so it would seem logical that some must be better suited for animal communication than others.

Chapter 5

The Giant Panda

12th. March, 1989

ust to set the scene, I will tell you that I was meditating with a group again, but as usual I was not always going where we were being led, because so often I get taken somewhere else, or something else happens as it did on this occasion.

I saw a really cuddly looking black and white bear coming towards me. It took me a while to decide what it was, as I have never really studied wild life. Eventually I realised that it must be a giant panda. I perceived it as content and happy as I watched it living in its own jungle type of environment. As I sat there admiring its beauty, it ceased to be alive. In its place, I saw a child's stuffed toy before me with similar colouring and markings. "Why aren't you real anymore?" I asked. "Because if you do not look after me, this is all that will be left", came the reply.

Chapter 6

A Little Interlude

Part One. Some Discoveries

One of the things that had been puzzling me right from the start was why did I become the receiver of these animal communications? The only quality that I possessed that not everyone has so well developed was my psychic ability. There are many far more efficient mediums on the planet than me, and probably thousands of naturalists would be able to recognise a tiger straight away, instead of needing the help with identification that I needed. To some extent, I still do not know enough of my own spiritual history, or soul history and origins to be able to understand it now. Nevertheless I did get some light on one of my other perplexities, and it could be connected to my choice of destiny in this lifetime. In fact it most probably is.

This other matter relates to both finding myself, and being found, "different". Sometimes in my life I had felt so totally ill equipped to cope with being a human being, that I would wonder if I could possibly be a walk-in. "What is a walk-in?" you may ask if you have not already heard about them. Well, as I understand it, it is someone who instead of being born here like the rest of us, could be an extra-terrestrial or absolutely anything, who by mutual agreement has stepped into someone else's body, as the someone else has left it. Such a person would surely feel totally lost having to cope with being physical in such a funny environment as Planet

Earth. With increasing frequency, I would feel frustrated that I did not seem to be able to operate in a body with a human brain etc., as well as I thought one should be able to. Then I had met Rhea Powers, since when I had had views of various incarnations on Earth, which seemed to eliminate that idea, so I forgot about it.

I was still tormented by this feeling of being different, and worse than that, having other people experience me as different, just as they had at school where they called me mad. I still felt laughed at, and not taken seriously. This kind of "Poor thing! She really can't help it," attitude was something that I was all too familiar with. In fact if anyone started laughing, and I did not understand what they were finding funny, I was always distressed by it. I dared to share this uneasiness with one or two of my spiritual friends during Rhea's Light Worker Training, but never found a solution. People would say, "Don't worry, you're normal." It made no difference how many times I heard these words, I was incapable of believing it, and therefore I could take no comfort from them. It was this very thing that made me unfriendly towards other people so many times. I would drive them away with aggression, or flee lest they get close enough to notice that I was not quite the same as the rest of humanity.

On 14th. March, 1989, something happened during a meditation at one of George Pratt's classes that made me even more suspicious. In brief, the exercise was supposed to be that under George's guidance, we would each return to our own home, where we would be greeted by an angel or guide. My home was actually about fifty miles away. We were to hold a small pebble or stone in our hands, and it was to be an eyes open type of meditation. I soon found that it was easier for me if I closed my eyes, and visualised the stone when necessary. The stone, (I had brought one with me that had been a present from someone who had found it on the beach near Findhorn), was to represent the Earth, and we were to visualise ourselves somewhere out in space gradually homing in on Planet Earth, then the country, then the area, the town, the street, and so on until we arrived at our own little home, and went in.

At every stage of this guided journey, I had great difficulty trying to go slowly enough, and was continually having to retrace my steps, as I kept on finding myself at least two moves ahead of George. While still out in space, I felt a strong urge to travel away from the Earth instead of towards it. I did as we were told, notwithstanding, and visited Earth. As I reached my house, I leant on the garden gate for a while before going in, as I thought that if I went straight in, I was certain to get ahead of everyone else again. Once in, I went straight to the room where I meditate at home. The lights were still out, just as I had left them. I then saw myself in the centre of this room carefully and thoughtfully building a wall. I could see that I was painstakingly putting each brick in place, and fixing it there with mortar. Some parts of the wall were higher than others, but that was because it was unfinished. This I feel represented my spiritual work and attempts at self-improvement, which must include all learning, by which I mean that no step can be left out. A brick missing at the bottom of the wall would weaken the wall.

Then George said, "...and you lean on the garden gate for a while before entering". I promptly left the house again in order to re-enter it on schedule. George continued, "You go to the house where you are expecting a warm welcome from someone". I went in, and found an angel in the house ready to fulfil the welcoming role. I was amazed to find out how put out I was at discovering that someone else had dared to enter my house in my absence. I thought that only burglars did that! "What are you doing here? This is my house! I am the only one who lives here". At the same time, the rest of me knew that I always welcome angels (unless I am doing something that I shouldn't), and the angel, who clearly understood all of this, looked faintly amused.

George said, "You knock on your door", and I knew that I had done it again, (got ahead), so I said to the angel, "Just a minute, I have done it wrong. It seems that I am supposed to be outside knocking on the door, so I will have to go out again". Out I went, and together we closed the door, so that I could knock on it for the angel to let me in again. The obliging angel opened the door, and this time reminded me, "Don't forget that you invited me, because you wanted someone here to open the door and welcome you". "Oh yes, so I did", I replied. We sat down together in my living room, and had a good laugh about it all. Next we went most of the way up the stairs to a point where I could see three spots of light, which were connected to each other making a triangle. Each of the three lights was situated in a room where I had received channellings from the animals. They were my meditation room, the room with the armchair where I like to read, and this upstairs room where I write it all down.

We went back downstairs into the living room, and just stood there in silence for a few moments, as George had decided to include a silent phase just then. Then there was a mutual consent between the angel and me to go somewhere else. We just took off together at a slight angle upwards, and left the house through the roof. We sped at the speed of our thoughts through space, and arrived on another planet. It was exactly the one that I had felt so attracted to when we were travelling towards Earth at the beginning. I had been to other planets before in this way, and this one was not unlike one of the others. It seemed to be existing on a different dimension to Earth. The surface of it was made of light. It had quite some depths to it, and I immersed myself into this light. I was surprised at how easily I could sink into it, and blend with it. I was in a state of pure bliss. I wanted to just stay there saturating myself with this soft soothing white golden light.

George was calling us back again. Very reluctantly, I put my hands on the shoulders of the angel, and we sped back into my living room. I then followed George's instructions to retrace my steps to the place where we had started out, which was the room with my physical body in it. We arrived ahead of schedule as usual, so I asked the angel if we could perhaps make use of the time with a quick return to the planet. (The angel was still with me by my request, as I had not wanted to return alone.) Hand in hand, and very rapidly, we arrived on this other planet again. I lay there basking in its light, which although not solid, was nonetheless denser than the surrounding atmosphere. The rest of the meditation group on Earth were starting to move a bit and stretch themselves. While I was so far away, my physical body was becoming hypersensitive, and I had acquired a slight ache around the solar plexus area, so I deemed it wise to return. I did not manage a direct route back, but found myself in the living room of my own house again, about fifty miles away still with the angel. As we stood together in the unlit room, I noticed that I was connected to the planet that I had just returned from by a chord of pure white light, which was running from my solar plexus. While I was standing there, I was overwhelmed by a powerful conviction that that was the planet to which I really belonged, and that on Earth I was merely a visitor. I had no desire to break the connection.

Returning to normal consciousness was difficult on this occasion. I managed it eventually, but for quite a long time, I felt rather absent, and was grateful that I did not need to try and speak to anyone for a while.

What strikes me as the most interesting information that came from this meditation as I look at it today, (nearly two years afterwards), is the build-up of light in the areas of my house where the channelling had taken place, and how these lights had connected to one another forming the triangle. Since then, I have noticed a considerable increase of light in this upstairs room where I have been writing it all out. I often become aware of the presence of the animals, or the trees, for example, while I am working on this book. It seems to me that they bring their light with them, and some of it remains here when they have left. One evening when I did not bother to turn the light on, as I merely wanted to put something in here, I could not help noticing how light the room was. Regardless of whether or not the light was on, I could perceive this other light from another dimension lighting the room. Just to be clear about this, I will explain that because this light was not of this dimension, I still needed the electric light for reading and writing.

Part Two. Verification and More Discoveries

When from the depth of my heart, I decided to step onto the spiritual pathway, and follow it into the Light, certain subtle changes took place in the energy field around me. It may be a gradual process with frequent relapses. I have learnt that the personality and the emotional body tend to become very addicted to the behaviour patterns that are familiar to them. This is certainly true for me. Even where the old patterns are causing personal pain, the personality/ego/emotional body hangs desperately onto them. This part of me finds change life-threatening, which slows down the process of transformation considerably if I let it, but it makes it a great challenge. What really keeps me trying is a combination of the challenge and the knowledge that this pathway leads to happiness. It triggers an awareness that no longer allows me to live in the old way with peace of mind. I know that I am never walking alone, even though this is hard to remember at times. It is as though a signal has been sent out to the rest of the Universe, which responds by providing me with every opportunity that I need at exactly the right moment in time. I may have no logical understanding of how things are working for me, but it is so.

In the Bible, Romans chapter eight, verse twenty-eight, it says; "And we know that all things work together for good to them that love God, to them who are called according to His purpose." I am becoming more and more aware of what this little quotation is actually about. I believe that it was in such a way, that just as I needed some help with the true implications of the previously described meditation to another planet, Rhea Powers had given my name to Linda Waldron in the United States before her visit to England. Therefore Linda had written to me telling me that she was coming, so that I was able to arrange a private sitting with her when she was in London on 16th. March, only two days after the mysterious meditation. I could not imagine that Rhea would have given her my name if it was not a good idea for me, so on trust, I went to London.

Linda Waldron is a trance medium who works mostly in trance, so that she can channel your spiritual guides, thus enabling them to answer any questions that you have. I arrived as requested with a list of questions. I gave her the jist of what had happened concerning the apparent connection to another planet, and asked what did it mean. While in trance, she spoke a great deal about this wonderful planet, and explained that I had lived there before this particular life on the Earth. Apart from being a place of learning, it is an evolved enough place to change the vibrations of those who dwell there. They vibrate faster, and extra colours are added to the aura. The chakras may also be altered, especially the heart chakra. (Chakras are part of the energy system of the body, and are recognised as such by yogis, etc.). When I later on asked for information on why everyone at school, for example, had found me different, and would I ever be normal, as I had tried really hard to learn how; Linda speaking personally to me said, "I can really sympathise and harmonise with that. I too have had that reaction my entire life." She told me that she had also lived on this other planet, and that her vibrations were just as different from other people's as mine were. People who are like this get called variously 'starseed', 'star person', or 'star child'. Linda thought that there were not very many of them, and that most of them were here rather reluctantly. She said that it was hard to find parents that were good enough to bring them up to their highest level, and some die in childhood, as they find it all too much. Others are prone to suicide, but those who survive all this need to make themselves available, and help in every way that they can. "You will never be normal", she told me, and as I sat there knowing that the person in front of me considered that the two of us were the same, for the first time in my life, I experienced being different as acceptable. In that instant I gave up the struggle to try and become the same as everybody else just to gain acceptance. A low profile seemed a good idea, but at last I was happy to be what I was. This was one of the greatest releases that I had ever experienced. Linda explained how people may sometimes feel this difference at a subconscious level, but they do not understand it, and it can make them uneasy.

When we discussed the animal channellings, she described that as my mission at the moment, and that she saw it as a book. I was really excited about this, as I had not considered that possibility before. Later in the year, while meditating, someone dressed in shades of green and brown with some light blue came and showed me a pile of five or six files, each one containing the material for a book. He told me that I would have a lot of work to do. So this was further confirmation for me that I must somehow put things together into a book.

Now that I had an explanation for why I felt so out of place on the Earth, in spite of having lived many previous lives here, I felt readier to carry out what ever my mission seemed to be. It was not all to be plain sailing though, as I was very prone to periods of doubt, dreadful cravings for a return to some other planet, and much frustration when things did not appear to be going as I thought they should.

Here is an example of an animal channelling which illustrates that last point.

Four animals approached me through the jungle. There was an elephant, a giraffe, a lion, and a tiger. It was still March, and not long since the giant panda's visit. They were repeating their constant plea for protection and consideration from mankind. Also, could we stop threatening their future existence by destroying their habitat, and so on. They found me fairly impatient, and part of the dialogue went as follows:

I replied to the above, "We all know that. We have known it for a long time now. You will have to give me something different if you want these things to be recorded. If they are virtually all the same, people will not want to read these communications."

The animals, "If you know of our plight, then why don't you help us more?"

"Men are too stupid." I replied, feeling exasperated and somewhat strained with my attempts to answer for the whole of humanity. Then, after a moment's thought, I slightly regretted my words and continued, "Well not entirely stupid, but they do these silly things out of ignorance. They are very short sighted, and act for their own short term benefits, which in the long term means first you leaving the planet, and then us."

The animals looked sad, and walked away. At first I had no intention of recording this little episode, but wrote it down sometime afterwards, just in case I should need it, and also because of an intuitive feeling that it should reach paper.

Chapter 7

...And So It Continued

As the animal channellings went on, I found that I experienced a certain amount of pain. Wonderful as they were, I could not remain totally switched off to the suffering and distress that seemed to come with them so often. At times, I would think to myself, "...but I don't want to bring all this sadness into the world. I would rather that I was channelling joyful messages. The World lacks joy, not sadness." Only gradually did I realise that the sadness, pain, and distress that came with the animals' cries for help was actually an expression of something that was already in the World, that could only be relieved if people became more aware, and took a deeper personal interest in the welfare of other creatures beyond themselves. In the long term, this would contribute to the evolvement of mankind, and would help to raise the level of consciousness in all creatures, as the soul level connections would either consciously, or subconsciously be strengthened. This realisation made it a little easier for me to be patient; and so it continued.

On 24th. March, an elephant came all on its own. Like the other animals it was appealing for help, and seemed to have a very special mission all about elephants. This was expressed as follows:

"Look at me! Do you not see how much light I bring with me? No other animal brings the very special energies to the planet that I bring. If mankind's acts force me to leave this planet, my energies can never return in their present physical form. No more will the light of the elephants shine on Planet Earth. I am one of the oldest animals on it. Many strains of my family died out long ago in the process of evolution. My kind, however, has survived. My beautiful ivory tusks appeal to the greed of men, and threaten my life. Have I survived so many changing ages of Earth' history, have I evolved well enough to survive, and still carry my light on the Earth, only to be eliminated by man's carelessness! Listen to the cries that come to you in the night. Bid men act while we still live. We have served men well for many years."

Flashes of light went out from the elephant on either side of him as he spoke.

It was two days later before I had time to write this communication down. I was concerned that I might let some salient point slip due to memory lapse. Therefore I reconnected with the spirit of the elephants before I started to write, and saw not just one elephant, but a whole herd of them following their leader through the trees. "We have travelled far." they said, "Do not let us down. Reach out and help us."

Two days later, I found myself disturbed by the nature of my recent communications with the animals again. Always the cries for help, and I merely recorded the pain, to pass on to others, yes, but it seemed as though I should somehow be able to do more. An idea came to me. It was a habit of mine to carry out healing meditations on what I considered was the off chance that they might be doing some good. So I did the World, then the rain forests, and why not a special one for the elephants? I thought. Where upon, having opened up my psychic centres, I started mentally sending out the thought, "I am sending rainbows of love from my heart to the hearts of the elephants." What I saw then was amazing. Before me were elephants dancing around, waving their trunks about, and screaming. It was a celebration. They had heard my message, and were rejoicing, and in their generosity were letting me see it. At the same time I noticed that the light in the rain forests was increasing, and so was the light around the elephants.

It would appear, that if enough light and love were sent out by everyone, there would be so much light in these places of need, that miracles really would happen. Furthermore, it showed me that there was something that we can do to help, and that even one person's help is greatly appreciated. Finally, I repeated this process for the Council of Animals, and watched the light in their circle grow.

Five nights later during my evening meditation, I was approached by a tigress. I had no fear this time, and when she had drawn close enough, I stretched out a hand and stroked her back. "I don't suppose you are used to the feel of a human forepaw on your back." I said half to myself, and half to her. No reply. She just took it all as though it happened everyday. I noticed as my hand slid over her back, that the coat was not particularly sleek. She was a little thin, and needed grooming I felt. I was sitting on the floor. In her dimension it was the jungle floor. She walked round behind me rubbing her body against my ribcage like a domestic cat. As she completed her little tour, she gave me a small nudge with her nose, and without words, I knew that I was to follow her somewhere. She walked away into the jungle without even turning her head. She knew that I was there obediently following behind her. She led me to a small clearing, and there was her litter of cubs. At some sign from her which was unobserved by me, they got up to join her. There were about four of them.

We made a turn to the right, and shortly afterwards arrived at a river bank. She led them down to the water where mother and cubs drank. She appeared to be playing with her forepaws in the water. She was catching fish. She opened them up for me to see. They were already half dead or unwell before she touched them, and inside they were discoloured. The water looked clear enough to me. There were no human settlements here, and no industry, but clearly these fish were suffering from polluted water. Somewhere upstream outside their habitat, the river was being polluted. Any animals eating these fish would therefore take the poisons into their bodies. She showed me the roots of the mango trees reaching down thirstily into the water."The trees will die." she said, "and see how the river water seeps into the ground on either side of the river poisoning the vegetation." She wandered round uneasily near the river bank, and around the place where she kept her cubs. Was this just a display of constant alertness that is present in all animals living in wild conditions? A simple way of tuning in to an unseen danger? No, it was more. I saw her cock her head a little to one side listening attentively. At last I realised what she was doing, and why she appeared so anxious. Although she was helpless to stop it, she was watching the edge of the jungle work it's way in closer and closer to her home territory, as mankind continued chopping the trees down. Soon she would have nowhere to live, and no clean water supply. The men would cease drinking the water when it poisoned them, but tigers had nothing else. "Why do your cubs need to drink water? Couldn't they live off your milk instead?" I inquired. "I did not have much." she replied, and walked away into the jungle.

Ever since I first started getting clairvoyant messages and visions both for other people and myself, I have always worried about whether or not I am getting the truth; and that if it is a genuine transmission, then have I interpreted that which I have seen, heard, or felt accurately. So much delusion is possible. Even one's own fear can cause distortion, or any other strong emotion, especially where one has an emotional involvement in the matter in question. On account of all this, I was very worried about the tigress having caught fish in the river. I thought that they only hunted on land. Since then, however, I have seen a tiger on the television doing the same thing, and since then, having also discovered that mango trees grow just how I had seen them, (another point which had been bothering me,) I decided that this communication was valid, and therefore would not throw the rest of this work into disrepute as well. Seeing things that I have none or little knowledge of, and finding out about them afterwards, seems to be part of my personal learning process, and the gaining of trust.

Chapter 8

A Horse At Last!

onsidering my involvement and interest in horses, it would not have been surprising if a horse had opened my animal communications. As it was, I had to wait until 8th. April, 1989 before one of those came along. I am sure, nonetheless, that the timing was perfect as usual. For not long after I had received it, I went to Germany to spend another week learning from Linda Tellington-Jones more about helping and training physical horses, and when she had read this, she persuaded me to read it to those of the group who were interested. This required a great deal of courage on my part, but with the comforting thought that at least Linda could accept it, and that she was sitting close beside me, I took the risk to please her. As it turned out, no one openly ridiculed it, and I believe that there were some who really appreciated it, and wanted more, so that the following day, I was persuaded to share some of the elephant communications as well. This was really a big step for me. Although some of the people present were at least a little bit experienced in esoteric matters, most of them were not. This experience gave me more courage, and has made it easier for me to share these things where interest lies in later situations.

It happened like this. After I had been meditating for a while, and was about to get up and go to bed, I saw the head and neck of a beautiful dapple gray horse. His exceptional beauty was combined with great strength and power. His large generous shining eyes had a highly intelligent expression. I had seen him once before, but on that occasion some weeks previously I was already in bed, and unable to prevent myself from falling asleep as soon as I saw him. "This time I must try harder," I thought to myself. "If he thinks that it is worth coming a second time like this, then he must have something to say." I looked directly at him, and waited.

"Touch me." he said. I stretched out a hand, and gently drew a circle on his forehead. "I love you," he responded.

"Why do you like to be touched?" I asked. "We need it. It helps to compensate for the manner in which you so often keep us. We see our friends, yet from our stalls, we can neither touch nor be touched by them. The feeling that we experience from the sensitive touch of a vibrant living human hand is truly wonderful. None of the inanimate objects in our environment can offer us this. It brings us to life. Through it we start to really live. Touch us."

I looked at him again, and saw what appeared to be a circle of light passing over his ears, and round under his gullet. Then I noticed that the upper part of this light ring ran right through the tops of his ears. I felt that I was being shown how the animal kingdom works closely with the realms of light. He was trying to show me how much they are tuned in to them. As I continued to gaze at this light ring, it changed from pale gold to all the colours of the rainbow. Although every rainbow colour was present, I saw that the healing shades of soft greens, blues, and lilacs were particularly prevalent.

While I was writing down this story, I again felt the presence of the horse close to my left shoulder, where he was sometimes licking the side of my neck, or gently nuzzling my neck or shoulder as a way of saying, "Go on, write it down. That's it."

Chapter 9

A Lion And A Badger

ometime during the night of 27th. April, when I was unsuccessfully trying to sleep on the back seat of the car of some very kind friends who were driving me from Cologne to Munich in the snow and driving sleet, a lion came to visit me. He did not stay long. He stood over my body, and I reached up putting my fingers into his shaggy mane to caress him as a greeting. "What do you want to tell me?" I asked. "My life blood is flowing down the river," he replied.

"Why is it doing that? How did it get into the river? Why on earth should it be flowing down the river?"

I found this piece of information thoroughly perplexing, and wondered if a motor-car was maybe not the best place to channel accurate information.

"I'll tell you some other day." answered the lion, and left.

I had a very long wait to get the answer to this. I knew that there had been a lion around me often. Frequently I had seen his face, but no words had been spoken between us. Finally I plucked up courage on 7th. December, 1990, and put the question to him once more. "Why was your life blood flowing down the river?"

The reply came not in words, for he showed me in pictures, and I felt certain realisations about them. This is how it went.

I saw the lion on the river bank. He was dragging his partially eaten prey along the ground. Looking at the shape of its feet, I decided that it must be a donkey, or perhaps a mule. I was certain that it was a domestic animal taken from a nearby settlement. On the other side of the river, I saw very clearly a dark skinned native with a rifle, who was shooting the lion, which is how his blood came to be flowing down the river. The tragedy of the story was that this was becoming a problem due to encroaching civilisation forcing the lions to live closer to the villagers, and with the decrease of their normal food supply of wild game, they were stealing out of need with increasing frequency, which was causing a culling of their numbers by man.

The lions are requesting more space.

The badger came on 9th. May, 1989 when I was meditating at home. I saw him in the middle of a wood. He ran out of sight for a moment, and then re-appeared holding a large white egg with a few grey speckles on it. I stared at him incredulously, as I know nothing about badgers taking eggs, and was already wondering if this was a valid story. The clairvoyant picture, however, was very clear, so that I could not mistake what I was seeing. Just after that, he broke it open, and proceeded to eat its contents. The yoke still looked fresh and yellow, swimming around in the white.

"It must have stolen the egg from somewhere," I thought to myself." In answer to the unspoken question the badger replied, "Men say that we steal, but if we do not help ourselves to food, then we die. It is done for survival. Leave enough space for us to live in."

Chapter 10
Elephants

here are people living on this planet belonging to the more aware sector of society, who believe that there are certain species of animals and plants, who sometimes elect to leave this planet. Their evolution here is complete. They may or may not be regarded as endangered species. For me this rings true, and I cannot see that any amount of effort put into trying to hold onto them could ever succeed in indefinitely delaying the working of this divine plan. Elephants may or may not belong to this group, but if they do, then it is clear to me that their time to leave the planet is not now. They still have so much to offer us, and they are crying out for the opportunity to stay here longer. This last conclusion is something that I have arrived at through their direct communication with me. Therefore I am going to share with you the following three communications.

While meditating in my own home on May 12th., I saw a man dressed like an Indian sitting cross-legged immediately in front of me. He was wearing fine clothes of beige, purple and white with a turban. His dark brown eyes were wide open, alert and sparkling, as though he really enjoyed every moment of his existence. He gave me the name of Patrick when I asked what he was called. Certainly, this was not an Indian name, but at least it was one that I could remember. Then there appeared a large elephant with him, one who apparently worked with and for mankind. I perceived other men around it, and it wore the most beautiful trappings, partly purple, and sparkling with jewels hanging down its forehead. I noticed that Patrick was holding a simple quartz crystal in his hand, and seemed to be directing energy from it towards my third eye. Afterwards I thought about that, and decided that he must have been using it to help me receive the transmission. I felt that the other men around the elephant were beings from the other side of life (death if you prefer), who were doing what they could to help support the elephants on this planet. Patrick seemed to be spokesman for them on this occasion. Then I drew closer to the elephant. In its trunk it took a pen, and on white paper wrote, "My name is Elephant." Someone must have told it about my difficulty identifying the tiger! It added,

> *"Don't be too slow in telling,*
> *Let the people know*
> *Before we go."*

I saw many elephants after that. They seemed to stay with me all through the night, waiting perhaps for me to put pen to paper the following morning. They appeared restless and uneasy, as though they were concerned that I might forget what they had told me, and fail to record it. Their continuous presence, however, was sufficient to keep all of it in my mind for long enough.

The second communication took place six days later in someone else's house, in fact at one of George Pratt's meditation classes. It occurred spontaneously after some other work. A white rabbit appeared sitting up on its hind legs just in front of me, obviously wanting my attention. Its ears were being emphasised more than anything else, therefore I assumed that I should be listening. He stepped aside to make way for an approaching elephant.

"Save us! Help us! Take action before we are gone, and it is too late. Imagine how it would be if you wanted us, but none of us lived on your planet. Each time that a species leaves, nature's balance is upset further."

At this point, a lovely bird of the jungle with beautiful colours and a long tail came into view sitting on a branch near the elephant's head. It looked agitated, and chirped out, "Write a song about it, or something". I thought it must be a bird of paradise, as I believed that they were brightly coloured birds, but a few years later a wild-life magazine revealed to me that it was a macaw. (By that time the German and Spanish editions had both published it as a bird of paradise, but the message remains the same.)

The elephant meanwhile, crying out about her beautiful ivory tusks, which appeared so luminous now, that I could not possibly miss them, was walking along a golden trail which led to a place of light at the end of the trees.

That last scene was quite incredibly beautiful to see. Although the animals did not attempt to explain the significance of this, I feel that the soft and beautiful golden light shown in that way, symbolises the light that means God, the light to which we all choose to return eventually. It is very obvious to me that the animals have souls and evolve. Death is not the end for them anymore than it is for us. I will give some of my reasons for believing that later in the book, when I come to write a little about my own horse.

When I returned home after this last meeting with the animals, I was keen to carry out their requests, and write out the song for the elephants. I made only one condition, and that was, that they must tell me what I should write, so that it really would be their song, and not something that I had made up myself. I sat down upstairs with pen and paper, and wrote out the title, "The Song of The Elephants", and waited. Nothing came, so after a while I decided that I would simply have to leave it. Meanwhile I received other communications from animals, which I will shortly recount, but nothing from the elephants. I had to wait two full weeks.

On 1st. June at home, I saw various animals approaching me, but the most prominent there in the trees, were two magnificent mature elephants; him and her, I felt. I watched them for a while, and then observed how they brought the colours of purple and silver-white. They turned a little more towards each other, as they had both been facing me, and whilst intertwining and playing with their trunks, they seemed to be talking to one another. As their heads drew closer together, I saw a ring of light that encircled both of their heads. It contained all of the warm earthy colours from bright red, through orange, yellow, and white to shades of green. Then, remaining still again, they spoke to me. It was "The Song of the Elephants". I was so excited, and realised after the first few lines as it started to come very quickly, that I would never be able to memorise it all without losing some, or a lot of it. I reacted by running up stairs with a handful of crystals to help me, reaching for pen and paper, and asking them if they could please start again from the beginning. They did, and I wrote it down word for word as I received it.

"The Song of The Elephants"

The wisdom that we bring

See the wisdom that we bring

Watch us and listen

We teach and you learn

We show you what we bring

With us you laugh and sing

We teach while you listen

We have something that men have lost

Since the Feast of Pentecost

Our simple wisdom, our knowing

Our knowledge and growing

But at present, oh sadness!

We are going.

I did not like the line about Pentecost, and wanted to leave it out, but somehow it did not seem right to start editing someone else's poem. Also, I cannot be sure that it does not hold some deep truth that should be left there. Of course, I never rule out the possibility that I might have made a mistake, but I will say that this is the best that I can do.

Now I was so thrilled that I had finally been given this thing after waiting two weeks for it, that I decided that I really must share it with Linda T.-J. It was nearly midnight here, but seven hours earlier for Linda, so I picked up the telephone to try my luck. Her assistant answered, and told me that Linda was in a meeting, her "Animal Ambassadors" meeting. I assumed that this was going to mean that I would not be able to speak to her that night, but to my surprise, the assistant decided to try and get her out of it for me, and Linda came. When I was about to recite the poem over the telephone, she asked me to wait a moment. I heard a click, and realised what she was doing, namely recording it. She said that she wanted to play it to the people in her meeting. Then I realised how it had come to me on exactly the right night. On any other night, those people would not have heard it. Perfect timing as usual, and it had nothing to do with me, as I had no idea of what was going on. Once again, I began to see that something much bigger than me was controlling these things.

Chapter 11

In My Garden

Providing the brightness of the sunshine does not put one off, and assuming that there are not too many biting, or tickling insects about, the peace and quiet of a garden can make a wonderful place for meditation. In fact, one can meditate anywhere, but places with good energy are usually preferable. Sometimes this energy comes from being with a group, especially when the group meets regularly, but my garden is also very good.

I had not gone out with the intention of meditating, but was just sitting there enjoying the sunshine, and looking at my flowers. I closed my eyes for a moment, and noticed how even with closed eyes, I seemed to be looking at still more flowers. I was watching a beautiful butterfly visiting one of them, when I noticed a tiger slowly advancing in the left hand field of my clairvoyant vision. I felt that he had not been far away, and that on observing me slip into a receptive state, he had decided to come and say hello.

When he was close enough, like an outsize affectionate domestic cat, he put his forepaws boldly on my shoulders, and proceeded to lick my neck and face with his mouth extremely wide open. First I ran a hand gently down his back, and then, just to amuse myself, I passed the arm of one of my more subtle bodies straight through him. I reflected on how even if he chose to close his powerful jaws around my neck, on this dimension, we could not harm one another. "This is what I really like," I told him, "meeting on this level, where neither of us has anything to fear from the other, and we can co-exist in peace together."

At this point the tiger removed his large paws from my shoulders, and having descended to a comfortable sitting position on the grass beside me, whilst looking slightly away from me with an incredulous expression on his face, he said,"I'm not sure that I really understand all of this". I comforted him by telling him that I was sure that he would come to understand it, if tigers ever needed to know about that, and I watched him walk away.

My next visitor was a crocodile some little distance away in the water. "I'm not keen on crocodiles", I thought to myself, for I felt that they were one of the World's least lovable animals. The crocodile had picked up my thoughts, and replied to them.

"We close our teeth on whatever we can find that will feed us. We kill to eat, don't you see? Without food we die. You think that we are devious, but if that were not so when we hunt, we would not be successful. We would perish. Leave us room to live as well."

Chapter 12
Learning Together

It seems to be widely accepted that most human beings are here on Planet Earth in order to learn. Some of them are conscious that that is what they are doing here, and others are not. Some are willing pupils, and others resent the whole process, although if they were to be regressed to the point where they chose this particular lifetime, they would know that no one has forced them to come. In fact we have all arrived here voluntarily for various reasons, or so I believe, if with varying levels of consciousness about it.

What about the animals? Are they learning as well? Basing my judgement on the communications that I have had, and also on logic, I believe that they are here to learn and evolve just as much as we are. Here follows part of my evidence.

On 7th. June, 1989, I was sitting cross-legged on the floor in the room where I usually meditate. Only this time, I had my cassette recorder placed just in front of me, also on the floor, and I was listening to a tape that a friend had lent me about metaphysical things such as expanding the consciousness and so on.

I noticed a leopard enter the room. He did not come particularly close to me, but nonetheless I reached out a hand and stroked him as a greeting, even though I knew that I intended to continue listening to the tape for the time being rather than to him. He first sat down, and then lay down, resting his head on his forepaws with half closed eyes. He did not as I had been expecting, make any attempt to distract me from the tape. The other animals arrived, as usual with only one representative from each species. When the white rabbit entered, it came bouncing past me, and then bounced back again, settling down as close to me as it could get on my right hand side with its nose resting on its front paws. I caressed his beautiful soft white fur, enjoying the wonderful love and peace vibrations which seemed to be present as the animals gathered. At last, we were all sitting in a semi-circle with everyone's attention on the tape. I noticed a domestic dog amongst them for the first time. Previously only jungle animals had been obvious at these gatherings. Later on I noticed a white cat as well. The dog did not sit, but stood with his head and neck protruding into the circle, remaining alert, as one might expect from the rough-haired terrier type of dog that he was.

From beginning to end, nobody moved. Only when the tape had finished playing did we disband, and I wondered to myself if I would ever have come to enjoy such wonderful company, if I had lived in a highly populated house in which there was no quiet place to go.

When I wrote these things down in the evening, I did it just as you see it above. Consequently, I had a second visit from the white cat the following day. I was seated in the same place listening to another tape, when it walked across the room with an air of self-contained dignity, and sat down on my right, apparently listening to the tape, one of a similar type to yesterday's. I enquired why it had returned this time, and although no actual words were used, the cat explained in a telepathic way, that yesterday's account of what happened had not been accurate where he was concerned. I thought about what I had written, and realised that I had made it sound as though the cat had been there at the same time as the rest of the Animal Council, whereas actually, he had come later the same day after the others had left, when I had returned to listen to more tape. The previous day had been a very brief visit from the cat. It had neither stayed long, nor sat down, or come close to me. It had been more like a piece of passing traffic! Obviously it wanted its presence to be noted, but not as one of the group.

Chapter 13

A Mermaid

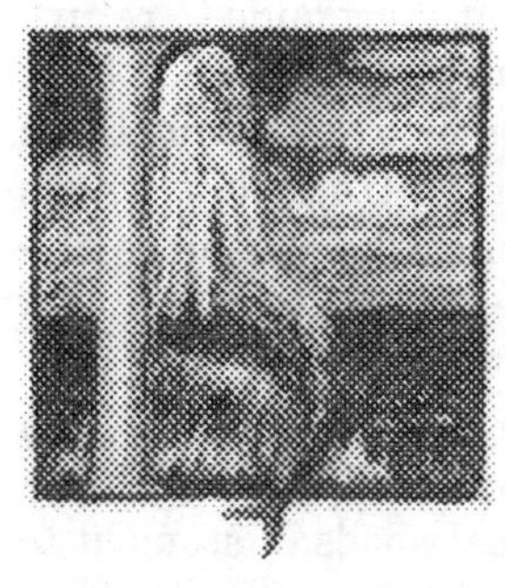

t happened in July of 1989. Late evening I was sitting meditating, when suddenly, there was this very clear picture of a mermaid in front of me. This was much more alarming than lions and tigers, because I felt confident that mermaids did not exist. What state of mind was I really in, I asked myself? I seriously began to wonder if I could be getting emotionally disturbed, and was this the result of spending too much time alone? I turned away from her, and found that I gained enormous relief when I could not see her any more. After a moment or two, I decided that it would be a good idea to take another look in the direction where I had seen her just to make sure that she really was not there. Rather warily I did this.

"Yes, I am here," she said smiling, with her lovely golden hair falling on her shoulders and back, her pale skin, and bluegreen fish-like tail. She appeared to be sitting on something, and although I could not see what exactly, she herself was so crystal clear, that I had to accept her as real. Then she left.

Chapter 14

Tree Experiences

t does feel good after mermaids to return to something as indisputable as a tree. Perhaps what I have to tell about them is more off the beaten track, but I have yet to meet anyone who disputes the existence of trees.

Towards the end of July when I was visiting my mother, I slipped out for a solitary walk in the woods. I stopped to talk to a tree. Putting a hand on its trunk, I began, "Hello! How are you?" "Happy", replied the tree. I was rather surprised, as previously I had only managed to find sad trees. "Why?", I asked.

> *"I am a tree in a wood,*
> *And it's good to be understood."*

I took this to mean that it enjoyed being allowed to grow freely amongst the other trees, and not be clipped or pruned like town trees and hedges. Remembering my own experience as a tree, and how upset and shocked I was when a man came along to cut me down without a word of warning or explanation, I bade this tree to remember, should the day come when it suffered a similar fate, that the men cutting the trees are too ignorant to go about it any other way, and not to forget that at least once someone had paused to speak to it, and tried to understand.

The next tree experience took place a few days later in my garden. I was sitting in the sun, and as I closed my eyes, at first I saw many beautiful flowers, but these were followed by a tree. The tree was unusual. It had a straight trunk with many lines on it, which then divided into three equal parts growing in three different directions. I perceived that this represented a three dimensional existence for the tree on Planet Earth, and that it's purpose, and also that of the flowers, was to bring light to the planet. They were manifesting God.

It is amazing what simple little things sometimes trigger off these experiences. For example in the next case, I was sitting indoors reading a book called "*Talking With Nature*", by Michael J. Roads. Expressed in my words, he spoke about the changing face of the Earth over thousands of years. He was saying how although the valley before him showed only a few trees, with his inner eye he was able to perceive how the valley had once been, and that it was filled with trees as a forest. It was like a shift back through time. I thought that this was a very interesting phenomenon, and I began to wonder what the area whereon my house was built, and also the surrounding territory, had looked like before man came along and made his mark there.

This wondering brought about an immediate spontaneous vision, in which I saw a large pine tree growing in front of the fire place. Where I was seated was earth and pine needles. Further away from this big pine grew other trees, many different varieties. They were not too close together, but positioned with spaces where the sun shone through between them. In some strange way, like a trick of time, it seemed to me that these energies were still present and accessible. I had always liked sitting in that particular part of the room, and if my chair was actually situated so close to such a beautiful tree, then no wonder that I liked it there.

Within a day or two of this last experience, I was practising one of the physical exercises out of the Arica Training called "pendulum", which involves standing on one leg, and doing things with your two arms and the other leg, and therefore requires good balance. That is something that I have never really had much of. I had been taught how to maintain my balance while doing this, but I still could not help wondering if there was anything else that

I could do as well to make it easier. I was indoors facing a solid wall, when I noticed a tree in front of me. It was perfectly still and steady with a beautiful straight trunk. My consciousness linked up with that of the tree, and I enjoyed almost perfect balance. This has only happened to me once like this. The tree was not physical, but had appeared just as the animals do.

Towards the end of August, I joined a group of Europeans from the Continent, who, organised by Giselheid McKenzie, were spending a fortnight in Arizona, U.S.A., the first week of which was to be a workshop under the leadership of the late Janet McClure, an American trance medium at the head of the Tibetan Foundation in the States. It seemed to me that when she was working, she followed the directions of Vywamus, (the entity who spoke to us to teach and help us all) as closely as possible. Although Janet was not too fond of the burning Arizona sun and heat, she obediently led us out into the sunshine, where we seemed to be wandering through part of Sedona's natural wilderness. We stopped by what looked to me like a fairly dead tree. That is to say an ancient tree, which had just a few leaves left at the top of it, but I would have loosely described it as "on the way out". Vywamus told us that this was an ascended tree, and asked us to stop and tune into it, and communicate.

The information and psychic experiences that at least three of us received were more or less identical. Between us, we learnt that the tree had lived for a long while successfully until the time came that the greater part of its essence ascended, leaving only a small part behind continuing a physical existence in order to be able to carry on helping the surrounding plants. We noticed that some of the tree's ascended essence was making a temporary return in order to help our group. During our silent meditation round it, I found myself drawn into the centre of the tree. This took place after I had made the decision to allow the tree to help me. For a moment, I felt like a part of the tree, and perceived its branches as branches of light reaching out into the atmosphere. Another member of our group had a similar experience with the roots. Next, I found myself being sucked upwards into the white light, which was part of the tree's essence. I felt that the tree was helping me to connect with all white light.

At the end of this meditation, and before we broke the silence by sharing our experiences, Janet McClure felt herself being asked to channel the tree. I am not sure whether Vywamus or the tree had asked her, but whoever it was, Janet expressed great surprise, and said that she had never been asked to do such a thing before.

I was amazed. Through Janet, the tree asked everyone to enter into its centre, so that it could help them to rise up into the light. In fact everything happened in exactly the same way as it had happened to me a few minutes earlier. When we spoke about it afterwards, I discovered that the rainbow of light which I had seen round the tree during this last part while Janet was channelling, had been seen by several of us. Before we left, we thanked the tree.

This is yet another of many examples, where I have had verification for my visions etc., something that I regard as a very necessary form of encouragement from time to time.

Chapter 15

The Rest of My Arizona and New Mexico Trip

he tree experience having taken me as far as my Arizona New mexico trip, I am now going to share with you what I consider to be the most interesting of the things that happened during that time.

It was the same morning as the ascended tree encounter. We made our way slowly through the natural vegetation near Sedona in the intense late summer Arizona heat. I suppose that we must have been about a mile from the town, and this unspoilt bit of land belonged with the private house that we had been allowed to use for our group meetings with Janet, thanks to the generosity of its owner.

We were moving downhill, and in a little dip, the people in front were quick to notice that the air was cooler, which made it a good stopping place for meditation. There seemed to be an empty stream bed, and we felt that there must still be water running under the ground, which would account for the cooler air. As we came to a halt, Janet observed that there seemed to be some kind of connection with animals there. At the same time I found myself looking at three zebras clairvoyantly, and they seemed to be approaching what in their dimension was a watering place, which was positioned immediately over the dip in the ground where we had first noticed the cool air. Then I saw other animals gathering with elephants and a rhinoceros among them. It was not just

Janet and I who were psychic, but also many others in varying degrees in our group. Therefore between us, we saw a great variety of different species, both large and small. At ground level I saw an energy vortex, a swirling mass of blue and white energy. Janet had seen this first, although I do not know in what colours, and through her Vywamus told us that this was an entry point to this dimension that the animals could use. Of course, there were other ways as well, but this was an easy way in. Shortly after that, Janet observed a small giraffe skipping up out of the vortex.

The animals asked me to speak for them, so with Janet's permission, I did. I explained to the group that they were all there, and quite visible to anyone with clairvoyant vision who cared to look.

"We have come for the benefit of your group", they said. "We are also *trying to evolve, and bring light to the planet. We can help* you, and you can help us", the animals concluded.

I was delighted and amazed. I had gone to the States in the hopes that the work with Janet would help me in my personal development, and to have had this wonderful contact first with a tree, and then with the animals all in the same morning had far exceeded anything that I had been prepared for.

"A Curious Meditation"

This was a meditation done in Janet's group work, but not one that I had any intention of writing down. Nonetheless, memories of it kept on haunting me like a recurring dream until I finally yielded, put pen to paper, and tried to write an accurate record of it.

We were sitting together indoors, and in my hands I held a snowflake crystal. It was quite large, and although my eyes were shut, I found that my inner picture was of my two hands holding this crystal. As I watched it, it was changing. Little by little, it took on the appearance of an elephant's head. The face was looking directly at me. It grew larger, and slowly an elephant walked out from the space between my hands, and stood beside me. I found myself lifted up, and placed astride the elephant. At this point, I wondered if perhaps my imagination was taking over, so I consciously shifted myself back onto the ground. My feet had barely touched the earth, when the elephant took me up in his trunk, and placed me back on top again. Satisfied, at last, that I was not inventing it all myself, I watched to see what would happen next. I found myself hovering horizontally face downwards along the back of the elephant. Our energies were mixing, interacting, and blending together. Somehow our relative proportions had been adjusted in such a way, that our main energy centres, or chakras, seemed to be perfectly aligned to one another. After a while, I was gently put back onto the ground, from where I watched the elephant walk away into the trees. (There had been trees all around us from the moment of his arrival.) Then I became aware that the snowflake crystal was looking its usual self again.

A few days later I asked Janet, (whose crystal it was), what special qualities did this particular crystal hold? She explained that it facilitated an entry point into this dimension, rather like a doorway. As far as I can remember, I had not told her anything about the coming of the elephant through the crystal at that point.

Janet was only with us for that first week, and consequently we had more time the following week for exploring other energy vortices, swimming in the river, visiting the Grand Canyon and so forth.

On September 6th. during this second week, a few of us rose early in the morning in order to watch the sun come up over the red Sedona mountains from a power point known as the Airport Vortex. There were a few 'normal' tourists wandering about with their cameras as well, but they kept well clear of us, so that we were able to meditate undisturbed.

Ever since I discovered that there existed something known as the Spiritual Pathway, I have always felt the urge to try and run down it in leaps and bounds, missing out anything unnecessary,

ME
LANZEROTE.
MY
NA

GO TO AFRICA →

and trying to get to wherever it led as soon as possible. Whenever I have wanted anything, I have never felt that next week would do, or that even next year, or the year afterwards would be all right, Instead, I want it all today, or yesterday would be better. In view of this, I should not have been surprised when a tortoise came and spoke to me as follows: "Walk slowly, and notice the little things", he instructed me. Shortly after this, I saw some other being in his dimension pick him up in an unfeeling manner, so I sent him some loving white light, where upon he was promptly returned to the ground. Opening his eyes really wide, he shook a couple of tears, and with mixed joy and surprise said, "When you send me light, it helps me to wake up," (spiritually). He repeated this last point a second time just to make sure that I took it in.

Shortly after this the sun rose. It did so amazingly fast. (In Europe, the whole process of sun-rising takes much longer.) So our little group started walking back for breakfast.

Later in the day, when I was trying to solve some personal problem, the tortoise appeared again, and said, "Don't expect to solve it all at once. One step at a time will be enough."

Altogether the tortoise had said very little to me, but when I looked at the content of it, I could see that it had really shared some wisdom with me, and I was left very thoughtful, as I tried to see how I could apply it all to my life.

"Boynton Canyon"

This is an area of natural rocks, vegetation, and a deep valley down the centre of it as far as I could see. It was a short car ride from Sedona, and therefore high on our list of priorities for our second week there. There are tracks where people can walk through it, and an expensive hotel which looks quite new situated at the entrance to the canyon. It is renowned for the feast of a breakfast that is served there, so we arrived suitably hungry, and enjoyed a delicious "brunch". As a fresh fruit, muesli-loving, and yoghurt-eating vegetarian, I found everything there that I could wish for. Armed with apples and water for mid-day snacks, we then set out to explore the canyon.

It seemed to me that it was all part of my learning process, that I must try and believe that the things that I see and hear and feel are fact, and not part of some self-devised fantasy. If I were to make the mistake of trying to interpret these things with my little human logical brain, instead of allowing my intuition to function, then I would really be going down a false pathway. However, nearly all of the things that I am about to recount to you were in some way confirmed and verified, either by the group, or by the guide who took charge of us.

After walking for some distance, we settled down on the ground for a rest. I had already noticed how thin the veil between the seen and the unseen seemed to be in this place. Only in certain special places by the Findhorn River in Scotland had I felt it like this before. The energy in the atmosphere was high. It also felt very clear and rather rarefied. Our guide told us that several ley-lines met there. As we sat down in a rough shaped circle, I began to sense the presence of animals around us. There seemed to be some unease on their part, and I felt that we were invading their territory. I reacted by sending them love, which changed the atmosphere, and brought them to terms with our presence. I had not said anything at this stage, but another member of the group said that she was sensing that a gathering of animals was about to take place, and sure enough they came. The larger animals came first, and with their non-physical presence formed a circle outside our circle.

Next I saw smaller creatures, and then a kangaroo. A large ant emerged from the ground to represent its kind, and then came a chorus of singing birds overhead, making a circle above the animals. Not where you would expect to find them, but high in the air I saw fish swimming about, that is around the circle, which intensified the energy. Giselheid told us of an angel presence which I was able to confirm, for there were many. Those of us who were able to tune into this gathering felt that it was a great coming together of different species, a time for integration, when our different energies could blend and mix, enriching all of us. We decided to celebrate this by standing up, and chanting "OM", which we did holding hands. When we were silent again, I observed that there was much jubilation amongst the animals. Then they seemed to disperse a little, some of them wandering through the surrounding trees nibbling the leaves, etc.. We humans were aware of a gentle settling down of the energies as things became still and quiet again.

Some of our group were not very fond of walking any distance, and especially not in the heat, whereas others, including myself, determined not to miss anything, decided to go on. We walked for quite a distance, mostly through the trees, so it was pleasantly shady. I was enjoying the soft pale blueish greens of the vegetation and the clean air. Finally we reached a good stopping place amongst the trees, from where one could glimpse high up on the hillside ancient Indian ruins in the red rocks. I had only just closed my eyes, when I felt the gentle touch of the hand of an Indian on my shoulder. He did not startle me, for I had seen him coming. He greeted me warmly, and then indicated the whereabouts of the rest of his tribe, who were gathering around us. Attached to a band around his head was a single white feather. "You were one of us once", he said to me. "We used to live up there." He was pointing to the aforementioned ruins in the rocks. "Are you sad that your tribes do not live here anymore?", I asked. "No, because our souls are at peace now", he replied and continued, "No doubt you will be going now?" most probably sensing a restlessness in me. "Not yet, because the rest of my tribe (I meant the group of course) are not ready to go yet, and I feel that I should stay with them." The Indians seemed to understand my feelings about that very well, so they sat themselves down close to the trees just outside our circle, and waited.

Meanwhile, I took the opportunity to explain to the rest of the group what had been happening. They received my story so well, and with such love, that the Indians drew closer to us." When you are open to us, we can come closer to you", their spokesman said. I passed this last comment on to the rest of the group, several of whom said that they could feel the warm and loving presence of the Indians as they drew closer." When you leave this place, you will not lose us, for we are free to go anywhere now." This we noticed, as I was aware of an Indian presence all the way to the entrance of the canyon as we returned to it. The trail that we followed had the typical slippery mixture of red earth and small pebbles that I saw so much of in the region. This combined with quite steep slopes to negotiate in some places, meant that in addition to good shoes, you really had to be careful not to slip and fall. As I slithered down a treacherous slope, a little Indian voice in my ear said, "The reason that you people have difficulty walking is because you wear shoes, so that you can't spread your feet out properly when you put them on the ground."

"At the Wupakti Ruins"

We had been to see the Grand Canyon, and on the way back we stopped to look at these Indian ruins. We wandered round them at a leisurely pace, until about four or five of us decided to linger behind in a part of them that attracted me. We started to tune into the area to try to see what we could learn about it. Fortunately Giselheid was there, as without her to confirm the things that I saw, I think that I might have dismissed it all as too unlikely to be true.

I saw many Indians all walking in the same direction, which was towards the sun in the west. The long grass and many beautiful flowers that they loved grew taller than their knees. "The flowers were all special", one of them said, "each one serving a different purpose." I understood this to mean that they had learnt the medicinal properties of each plant, and anything else that they could be used for as well. Next I saw what they were really heading for. It was a rectangular pink space ship, which, supported by fairly short legs at each corner, was able to sit lightly on the ground. Although it was not transparent, I did feel that had I stood beside it, then maybe I could have put my hand straight through its fabric. It was as though it were made of dense light. Perhaps one could describe it as half physical, and its shade of pink was almost identical to that of my pink tourmaline crystal.

From it, there stepped out some silvery-white beings, also only half physical, and nearly see-through. Each had arms, legs, head, and body, but no proper face. The antennae on their heads were quite short, and their bodies rather angular, almost rectangular rather than rounded like ours. We were clearly seeing a scene of the past, and yet these characters were present once again to help explain to us what was happening, and later to answer questions. In a way, it almost proved the non-existence of linear time. They were as much in our present as we were in theirs, a time that one would normally call past, with our present being their future, and yet both were the same moment. The Indians rushed towards the space people with trust and friendship. I wondered what was going on, and understood that the Indians were learning from them how to ascend. Meanwhile, I was relating all this to the others as it happened, but when I got to the bit about ascension, I did not dare say it, so I told them, "The Indians are learning something from the space people", whereupon Giselheid put in, "What I'm getting is that they taught the Indians how to ascend". It seemed unlikely that we had both got it wrong, especially as Giselheid had not heard me say that first. Reassured by this, I found the courage to say that this is what I thought as well. Of course it is much easier to make these bold statements, if someone else has just said it!

I put various questions to both the Indians and the space men as requested by one of our group.

"Why did you decide to leave Earth in this way?"

"We had done everything. We had no reason to stay here any longer", replied the Indians.

"Where do the space people come from?"

"We come from a planet of love."

"Will you come again?"

"Yes, but we cannot tell you when in your terms, but when there is havoc on the Earth, we will come and help."

I saw them waving goodbye to us, and starting to withdraw to their spaceship. We sent out love to them, and thanked them.

This is really just as much Giselheid's story as mine. It was simply that for the most part, I spoke out loud what I was seeing, while she was receiving the same in silence.

Afterwards I began to catch up on the known history of the place and people. I discovered that it was quite a popular belief among esoterics, that the Indians who had left this place had done so by ascending. On the other hand, those who do not accept such things say that it is a mystery, and that all that is known is that at a time when the land was fertile there, and when they had all that they needed to live, a whole tribe of Indians mysteriously disappeared at the same time, and no one can say where they went. When we visited the area, it was all like a barren desert, apart from a few tough looking bits of scrub growing there, but in my vision it was fertile with long grasses and flowers. There had even been some small trees in the background. So what had happened? I was soon to find this out. At one point in its history there had been a nearby volcanic eruption, and the rich larva which flooded over the land gave it some years of fertility.

New Mexico

The two weeks in Sedona came all too soon to an end, so I embarked on the final lap of my trip, which was to take me to New Mexico where I visited Linda Tellington-Jones. Linda lives in a small village north of Santa Fe, and from there she drove me up into the mountains. Part of the way up one of them, she stopped the car, and we got out to go and sit beside a beautiful little mountain stream. I knew that the idea was to meditate, so I closed my eyes, and took a look to see if anyone was there. Almost immediately I saw a mermaid, and beside her a large sunflower. She greeted me without words. Her tail was greenish in hue, and a little later, I became aware that she had company. Her companion had strong red colours in his tail. I found that these two shades together seemed to have a balancing effect. It definitely felt like a him and a her, but I never managed to see his face clearly, so I was simply left sensing this. The only thing that they said to me was, "We are here again." It was as though they were trying to show me that my first encounter with a mermaid had been no fluke. I mentioned their presence to Linda, whose mind seemed to be elsewhere, as she did not react in any way to this. I knew, however, that I really trusted her, and that I felt completely safe sharing it with her.

Shortly afterwards, still with closed eyes, I saw a snail close to the bank of the stream.

"Wouldn't you like to be a snail?", it enquired. "Just think, you wouldn't feel the need to take those big leaps that you find so taxing on your courage anymore. You could just crawl along slowly and gently feeling totally secure. You would carry a lightweight house on your back onto which you could retreat at the slightest hint of danger. Now wouldn't that be nice?"

I almost felt that the snail was trying to carry on with me where the tortoise had left a few days ago. At least it gave me something to think about. I shared the snail story with Linda, who replied, "You mean you are seeing all that now?" as though she had thought that up until then I was recounting past experiences. I gave her an affirmative, and by request, looked to see if anyone else was there. Sure enough there were two large elephants standing on the opposite bank of the stream. They had come for the sole purpose of talking to Linda. I never wrote down what they said, as it seemed to me that that was Linda's private message. However, I do remember how Linda enjoyed it when I told her that they were trumpeting away with pleasure when they liked something.

Following the elephants came the Lord Maitreya, one of the ascended masters, not for me, but to speak to Linda with words of love and encouragement, and when I saw that the hands of his companion bore the stigmata, I thought that Jesus must be present, but said nothing in case I was wrong. Then afterwards Linda told me that usually when other psychics had channelled the Lord Maitreya for her, they had also found Jesus standing nearby. That was the confirmation that I needed in order to tell her that he had been there for some time. I learnt that this mountain was a place with a reputation for such channellings, which is why Linda had chosen to take me there.

13th. September was my last day in the States. Linda was still suffering from jet-lag after her return from Europe, and as she had been away for quite some weeks, she was heavily overburdened with work, so I went for a walk in the hills near her home on my own. Linda had painstakingly drawn me a little map to help me get started in a suitable direction, but once I reached the final frontier shown on the map, it was up to me to try and notice a few land marks, and avoid getting lost. This has never been my strong point, and many times my various horses have had to carry me miles further than I intended they should while waiting for me to get "unlost". This time, however, it would be my own legs that would suffer if that happened.

It was very hot, so having travelled some way, I sat down on a rock near an empty river bed. "Why do I feel like a little boy?", I asked myself. I was feeling smaller than my real size, and decidedly boyish. Looking to my right with my inner eye, I found the answer. A little boy was sitting beside me, and I had been sensing his energy before I saw him. He told me that his name was Owen. "Why are you here?", I asked. "I have come to stop you getting lost", he replied with a marked American accent, which was enough to convince me that he probably knew the land. His guidance turned out to be very useful. On my return trip, each time that I felt unsure of the way, I called to him, and then my head would seem to turn automatically to the direction that I should be walking in in order to return to Linda's house.

Actually, that was later. Before returning, after I had rested on the rock for a while, I decided to climb up higher, and kept on going until I reached a rock to which I felt particularly attracted. I sat down there, and with closed eyes began to look around. The first observations told me something that I had already guessed, namely that the land there had once been much more highly populated with Indians. Then the Indians that I was looking at faded from view, and for a moment, I thought that I was alone again just sitting there on my chosen rock. Then in front of me, I saw a single Indian. He was looking intently at me, and showing me crossed arrows. I had recently learnt that this was a sign meaning friendship amongst Indians, so I welcomed him. He brought with him a loving and warm vibration. He felt to me like a truly evolved and spiritual being. If this was so, then why was he still roaming the hills like some recently deceased earth-bound lost spirit? Why had he not moved away from this reality to realms of light in order to further his own evolution? It seemed so strange to me that I decided to ask him about it.

"We have moved on", he replied, speaking not only for himself, but also for others like him. "These are what we call our working clothes", (referring to his identity as an Indian). "It is done to give you a reference point. Our purpose in coming here is to help with the re-integrating of mankind with the rest of creation here on the Earth; animals, plants, rocks, and so forth. The Indian in you will re-awaken." He put his hands together letting his fingers interlock to illustrate the integration, this coming together of humanity with everything else. I wanted to talk for longer with him, but he had delivered his message, signalled with his hand that our communication should cease now, and resolutely started walking away from me. "At least stay long enough to say goodbye properly", I implored him, feeling rather desperate about it, and wondering what sort of an Indian farewell would be suitable. He turned towards me again just for an instant, appreciative of my needs. With a twinkle in his eyes, he blew me a kiss over his shoulder like a westerner. I sent the same to him, and he was gone.

This man had really given me a message. He had enabled me to understand why the animals were coming to speak to me, and all the other beings like trees, and so on. All of this was part of the coming together of the different kingdoms. I knew that mankind could not continue with the widespread separation that currently exists. This had not been an animal communication, but it explained to me the significance of my channelling of all these different aspects of consciousness. A wonderful finale for my Arizona-New Mexico trip.

Chapter 16
Africa or Not

hile I was still in New Mexico sitting beside the mountain stream with Linda, she made some reference to what we would be doing in Africa later in the year. I knew about the group of people whom she planned to take on a wonderful trip to Kenya starting on 28th. November, but I had decided against joining them. Firstly there was something else that I wanted to go off and do at that time, and secondly, it was a lot of money, and thirdly, money does not grow on my apple trees. So I told Linda that I was not coming, that I had not ever planned to come, although I had inquired about it once, and that I was expected elsewhere during that time.

"But the animals are saying that they were sure you were coming. They always knew that you would come!", exclaimed Linda drawing on her own channelling ability. I felt dreadfully torn inside. I had two friends both leading groups that would surely be helpful to me, which would take place at the same time. On the one hand, there should not be any choosing to do, because I had already made a choice, and that was not Africa. Anyway, I was scared of the unfamiliar insect population that I might meet out there, and perhaps I would pick up some dreadful kind of African illness, and have a miserable time. My other plan felt safer, and probably more useful for my spiritual development I thought. Linda seemed to at least partially understand my predicament, but two days later as I said goodbye to her on her doorstep, she begged me to try asking the animals what I should do.

I hate making decisions, and this was no exception. The whole thing seemed so difficult, that I frequently tried to push it away from me, and simply concentrate on living my normal daily life in England. Unfortunately I had this nagging feeling that refused to leave me whatever I did, that I must somehow face it, and decide if I would leave things as they were, or change everything and go to Africa. The internal emotional conflict was the worst. It seemed to be eating its way into my solar plexus mouthful by mouthful. I would have to resolve this, and preferably soon, before it was too late to make a change if I needed to. "Ask the animals", Linda had said. I did not like that idea, just in case they were biased. In fact, I was deliberately avoiding all contact with them, because I wanted to be able to reach my conclusions without the influence of such "interested parties".

Finally one afternoon at home, while I was cleaning my house, I thought to myself, "I would give anything, absolutely anything, if I could only find someone else who could make these decisions for me. I have had enough!" "We will!", came ringing through the atmosphere loud and clear. It was all of the animals shouting at once. "Who let you in here? You are not supposed to be in here just now!", I told them. "How did you get in?" Well, that was the end of that conversation, but realising that I could not hold the animals at bay for much longer, I made the decision to meditate on it that evening, and to ask for advice from my spiritual guides or the angels. My only ambition was to seek out the best possible spiritual pathway, and to follow it. I sat down and asked.

As I opened my inner eye, I found myself looking at the planned programme, which I knew would eliminate Africa if I stuck to it. The picture of it was a little to the left, and I could detect a strong pull in that direction. I knew that it was easier to go there than to resist it. Then to the right, I saw another pathway which seemed to be going much further. It was more brightly lit, which seemed to suggest that it was the intended way for me to travel. Nonetheless, it did not appear so simple, because there was a huge boulder blocking this path. As I watched, an angel appeared, and pushed the boulder to the side of the path. "Go to Africa. Go to Africa." The command was coming strongly, loudly, and clearly from somewhere just behind my left ear. Now I saw five or six angels spread out along the pathway, and they told me that they would be with me for every step of the way. "Does this mean that I will be spared all illness, or any other physical damage?", I asked. "It means that all of your spiritual needs will be looked after", came the reply. When I thought about it, I realised that this was all that mattered, and agreed to accept the terms. I made the necessary re-arrangements, and went to Africa.

In between making that decision and leaving, I was mostly very busy, which as usual meant less time for meditation, and less opportunities for the animals to reach me. While still at home on 2nd. October, however, I saw some giraffes coming towards me. "Don't cut them off!", a voice from nowhere cried out just as I was thinking that I could not cope with them. "Yes. We have got something to say to you", replied one of them to my thoughts. The voice was amazingly deep. "We have very long and beautiful necks. When you want to know how to use your neck properly, call on our energy, and we will help you. Notice also how we relate to our young. Notice how we reach down to them touching their bodies in many different places. It not only helps to bond them to us, but it is like having early lessons in bodily awareness."

I thanked them, and told them how beautiful they were, and the conversation closed.

Chapter 17

The Trees and the Little People

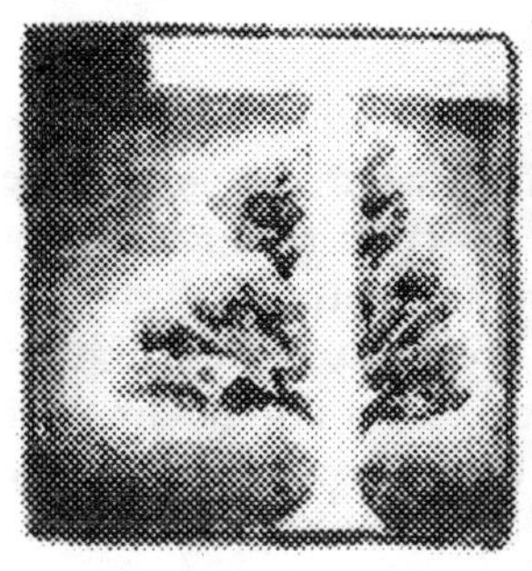

his chapter is an account of two little stories of what happened in between my U.S.A. visit, and Africa. The first of them is a tree story.

On 24th. September, 1989, I was in the middle of a type of meditation that I was trying for the first time, when I started to go off at a tangent to the planned track of events, just as I was connecting with the energy of a tree. In my sitting room there are no trees on a physical dimension, but those from other dimensions are free to come and go as they please. Maybe they are always there, one or two of them, but I am not always aware of it. The tree started to show me things and speak to me. I was perceiving its light body most strongly. I was being shown how trees are channels. The roots of the tree reach down deep into the earth spreading themselves out making the tree above ground stable, and enabling the tree to be nurtured by Mother Earth.

Next it was pointed out to me, that this is how a good human channel should be, really well grounded, and connected to Earth. Then there were the branches, all represented as lines of light reaching upwards to the sky, and drawing down the light from above into the being of the tree, into its channel; just as light can be drawn down through the chakras of a human into the human's channel, as well as wisdom, or anything else that you wish to receive. Finally the middle section of the tree had its branches reaching out horizontally, and they were channelling out light, energy, and other qualities into the physical dimension, some of which reached the other surrounding trees. In this fashion, the tree could serve the earth-plane by acting as a link between the two dimensions with all the pervading light, which penetrated its being from the tip of the highest twig to the extremities of the most far-reaching root. I could see that the tree was perfectly adapted to do this, and that we could and should function in a similar way. This tree was an oak tree, and was channelling the qualities most compatible with itself. Other trees and plants operate in a similar manner the tree told me, each a little differently according to its species.

I began to see the importance of channelling out what you receive, otherwise the channel could become partly clogged up, or nearly cease to function, whereas letting things flow right through allows the channel to be kept clear, and in good working order. This observation seems to hold true whether it be light or information that is being channelled. With information, if no one is there at the time to pass it on to, I have found that I can release it by writing it down, so that it can be stored externally instead of clogging the mind, which otherwise in my case keeps on trying to hold on to it.

I also noted when looking at the tree, that its channel was extremely open at the top, thus providing an easy passage way, so that the tree's consciousness could pass in and out of the tree as required, or at will. It was just as true that light could pass through this broad channel easily.

The second story took place in Germany. I was just there for the week-end, as there was a Feldenkrais workshop being run a few miles north of Hamburg. Although it must surely exist in England, I had not seen any advertised at that time, and my curiosity was great, especially as I knew that Linda T.-J. had done a lot of work with it. Due to the flight times, I arrived there long before anyone else the preceding day. It was 10th November, and a rather wet and cold afternoon, but as it was still light, I decided to take myself for a walk. There seemed to be plenty of tracks away from the main road, and the landscape was a mixture of fields with little patches of woodland here and there. On my return to the centre where the workshop was to be held, some intuitive urge prompted me to explore a small path leading into some trees. Standing under a large pine tree, I was grateful to rest for a while from the wind and rain. It grew on the edge of a small grassy clearing in the trees, which was peaceful, and beautifully sheltered. I closed my eyes, and became quiet.

The place was full of little people. They seemed to be grouped all around me. They were not all the same, but I gathered that all of them had some kind of connection with nature. Some were nature spirits to the trees, others to the grass. Others looked more how I would imagine gnomes to be. In some strange way, they seemed to exist in a different kind of time span. I learnt from one of the gnome-like beings, that over the last two hundred and fifty years or so, nothing much had changed in their existence, whereas I knew that mankind had grown and changed a great deal in that time. The difference in the rate of events and change seemed to be the cause of the different conceptions of time passing. Two hundred and fifty years ago was like yesterday to them.

"Men grow further and further away from us", he said, and continued, "Most of them simply don't see us at all now. They have separated themselves from us with their pace of life and busy minds, plus the arrogant belief that they don't need us, and that we aren't even there. Yet this is sad, because if there were contact between our two dimensions frequently, it would help mankind to understand us and our workings, enabling a happier co-existence to come into being. At one time we touched man more, but most of them have forgotten us now, and we prefer to dwell apart from them. Such a union would also advance our evolution, as it would bring us into contact with the higher emotions of man. The children come here sometimes, and play their games around the trees. This we enjoy, and we linger around to watch them. Sometimes they can almost feel our presence. If only they would open their minds just a little more."

I thanked the little people for this communication, and the trees for their lovely reviving energy, while I drew in light, and channelled it out to them. I took my leave of that place with a feeling of upliftment, in spite of the sadder aspects of the little people's message, for I felt refreshed by the energies of Nature.

Chapter 18

Africa

By The Camp Fire

inda's Africa trip started with a night in Nairobi, and continued with about twelve nights living in tents 'on Safari' while we rode horses over the Loita Hills, and finally ended up in a camp beside the Mara River. Following that we spent two nights in Mombassa, from where we set out on a snorkelling expedition on the second day, after which we returned to Nairobi, and then flew home again.

One of the things that I enjoyed about the camps where we spent the nights on Safari, was that no matter what time of day or night it was, there was always a camp fire burning. It was there to greet us at six thirty in the morning when we emerged from our tents for a cup of tea or coffee, and there would be another one waiting at the next camp when we came riding in, be it mid-afternoon or evening. I came to love the smell of it, and the bread which the African staff cooked for us on the camp site smelt of the camp fire as well. It was delicious. The daytime was usually very hot, but in the evening the temperature would drop, and then it was lovely to sit by the warmth of the fire. Evenings were also dark. It only stays light for about twelve hours each day, which meant that from about seven in the evening onwards, we were using oil lamps. Usually after the evening meal we entertained ourselves by sitting round the fire story-telling. When we asked our guide questions about life in Africa, we found ourselves with a very gifted story teller.

When most people were wending their weary way to bed, Linda put word round in soft tones that if anyone was interested, we could have a meditation circle round the camp fire. I was interested. There were sixteen people on the trip, but only a few of us gathered by the fire now. I never wrote these things down at the time, as I did not think that I would need them for my book, but I can see now that some information on what happened would help to add to the picture of how things work.

Not surprisingly, the animals came round. I particularly remember how there were about three zebras who arrived in the middle of our circle, and then made their way round to Linda. They went all round her, and I saw one of them rubbing itself affectionately against the back of her neck. As I often do, I was sitting there wondering if these things were really happening, or was I just a good story teller? After all, it would not take much imagination to work out that when someone does as much for the animals as Linda does, then of course the animals would want to go and see her. I was not left wondering for much longer, as Linda suddenly said, "Oh yes! I can feel them!" (referring to the zebras.) This was such a help to me, as it seemed to validate everything that I was doing. I noticed the Lord Maitrey standing some distance behind Linda, but I did not give his name, in case I was wrong. He seemed to be there to encourage Linda with her work, just as the animals had acknowledged her.

The next bit was really hard for me, and I channelled it to the whole circle with great reluctance. "I have got someone here who wants to talk to you", I hesitantly began. I knew very well who I thought it was, but was very loathe to reveal the name. I was too concerned about what this group of people who I had only just met, apart from Linda, would think of it all. Anyhow, who was I to channel Jesus? They would surely jump to the conclusion that I was some kind of heretic, or an evil witch pretending to be something that I was not. I tried to get round the problem by just channelling the philosophy as an anonymous message from somebody, but this was not to be. I felt so much pressure to reveal the name, that I finally had to reveal it. Such a being as Jesus would hardly need the recognition of who he was, so either this was a test for me or else it was felt that the group needed to know in order that they could understand where it was all coming from. This was twelve months ago, but I remember still that it was a description of his work, a little of what he is doing now, and most important, how his energy can be reached by anyone, and that he was/is available for any need. His evolved being was something much larger than most of us imagine and therefore he is able to give help in many places simultaneously, so that no one need feel when they call on his energy, that they might be depriving someone else in greater need. It does not work like that.

When I had finished speaking, Linda said a few things to the group about what I had been doing, which I found helpful, as it made me feel more comfortable about the whole thing. Nobody challenged me on the validity of it, for which I was truly grateful. In bed that night, I was aware that I had channelled something much more powerful than usual, for I found that all of the different realities that I perceived were swaying to and fro. I was relieved that all that I had to do was remain lying down, and drift into sleep.

The Spirit of Africa

It was mid-morning, and the sun was very powerful. We were riding our horses across the open expanse of the African plains. There had not been rain here for ages by the look of it. The grasses underfoot were burnt up and dry. With so much space at our disposal, it was not a surprise that we had spread ourselves out over quite a broad area, and although we were all heading in the same direction, it was possible to be alone with one's thoughts. Although our ride was punctuated with short bursts of speed, most of the time we rode at a peaceful walk, so that I needed very little of my attention on the horse, whose main aim seemed to be doing his work as required. Some of the way, I thought about life, and the trip that we were enjoying, and some of the way my head was just empty. One tends to think less in the heat I find. Sheltered from the worst of the sun's powerful rays by breeches, long leather boots, longsleeved shirt, hat, and gloves, I started to try and attune to the energies of my environment.

I perceived a presence in the sky. It vaguely resembled a face, with the rest of what ever it was situated around the face. It was white and light blue mixed together, and it blended well with the sky, although it did not exist on a physical dimension.

I put the question very directly, "Who are you?". This was when it became difficult for me, because I confused the voice of the being in the sky with that of a discarnate human-being, who happened to be trying to reach me. When the reply came, "You can call me Edward if you like", I assumed that it was the thing in the sky that was answering, so instead of addressing the man who had spoken, I told the thing in the sky that I felt unhappy about calling it Edward. Somehow it simply did not fit. Anyway, convinced that I was not dealing with anything human, I decided that such a name must be false. The next reply seems to have come clearly from the thing in the sky, and not from Edward. I felt so certain that what ever it was had never been called Edward before, that I continued, "Yes, but who are you? What are you? and where are you from?".

"I am the Spirit of Africa. I belong to the whole of this continent. My roots sink down deep into the earth. Those who wish can feel my energy as it rises up into their beings. Just open yourselves to it, and it will fill you, and move you. With this energy you can run for miles without fatigue. There are those among the Massai who understand these things."

The above reply I could accept. It felt like a clear and truthful communication. I realised that the Spirit of Africa was something existing everywhere out there, although I think that it is easier to feel it out on the plains, or in the hills, or in the bush, than it would ever be in a town, as in towns there are so many other vibrations coming from the people and the buildings.

Edward?

So what about Edward? It took weeks before I managed to work out what had happened with Edward, by which time I had handed out two rather muddled accounts of my contact with the Spirit of

Africa to friends, in which Edward and 'it' shared the same identity. The clues that I needed eventually came to me thanks to Edward's persistence. He knew that I was never going to try to reach him, and therefore had to take these opportunities to get a word in when he found me open, even if it did result in a muddled Spirit of Africa. His next attempt took place in Mombassa.

I was trying to do some channelling for one of the group. Again came the name Edward, but with the difference that this time I did not mistake him for part of Africa, but knew that I had a man visiting me who was fairly tall and slim. He managed to make me realise that he was nothing to do with the person whom I was trying to help, therefore I knew not to mention his presence. Meanwhile I was telling my 'client' about her dog whom I could see very clearly, and was able to describe him well enough for her to know him. Then I mentioned a little brown terrier-type dog, who was not relating to her dog, but came trotting across the clairvoyant picture that I had. This dog meant nothing to her, so I thought, "Oh, it must be some stray who is here by mistake". Nothing is by accident, but I forgot that as you will shortly learn. I still had not realised that Edward had anything to do with the name that I had picked up whilst I was riding, or that the dog had anything to do with him.

Edward's next attempt took place weeks later. I was back in England, and driving myself home from work having attended to my own horse as well. I do not recommend that anyone tries anything so stupid as meditating while driving, but that was not my intention, and neither is it the first time that someone has managed to reach me in this way. I was not meditating, but trying to concentrate on driving the car. I knew the road well, and I suppose that my brain was not very busy just then, as I heard the name of Edward ringing in my ears. "Edward again!", I thought to myself, "What ever is this about?". Edward was repeated, and then the name of Ben. I was just wondering what the name of Ben had to do with all this, when suddenly the truth dawned on me. "Are you my Uncle Edward?", I asked. "You really should know by now. I have been enough times", he said sounding just a touch exasperated. "And was Ben your dog then?", I continued. "Yes". At last I had it. Uncle Edward had followed me across the plains of Africa to try and get a word in. His presence having been acknowledged, he tried again in Mombassa, where he brought his dog, but I still did not get it. A third attempt, and at last he was through.

I still had something that I did not understand. I felt sure that he had had two dogs, both of them little brown Norwich terriers, although I could not remember the name of the second one. Now it gets really intriguing. My aunt, having heard through my mother of the re-appearance of her former husband, decided to telephone me in order to get the facts first hand. She was not really into this sort of thing, and wanted to know if I really believed that we meet up with our favourite pets after we die, and do animals go to heaven anyhow? I explained that to the best of my knowledge, where there was a love-link, there need be no separation, as the love would draw man and animal together. This holds true for people as well. My aunt wanted to know why the second little dog, "Boy" had not been there as well, but when I told her about the love link being necessary, she was able to answer that question herself. She explained to me how Boy had hated all men. He was very afraid of them, and had even growled at my uncle, which can't have done much to improve their relationship.

Edward seems to be happy that I finally had this conversation with his wife, and did not need to come again. Perhaps I should contradict that by adding that I have felt his presence while I have been putting this story together, and he seems to be very happy about it.

Team Work

Back in Africa on 8th. December, about half way through our trip, we stopped the horses for our lunch break. Having made them comfortable, tied up the potential deserters, and left the others free to roam and graze where they pleased, I ate my picnic from my saddle bags, and then settled down on the grass for a siesta. My intention was to sleep, but as I closed my eyes, I sensed an animal presence. I looked carefully, trying to identify what was there, and gradually the image on my inner field of vision became clearer. It was an elephant, who seemed to be standing in a silver coloured paradise. There were others behind him, but he was the speaker. "We are a team", he said. "We work together as a team." He was indicating with his trunk, that the rest of the team were the elephants behind him. I watched him as he advanced and arrived at a stream. With his trunk, he drank from the crystal clear water, and then squirted some over his body. "We are trying to find ways of helping raise the awareness level of mankind."

They did not tell me what methods they were actually using, so I was left to fathom that out for myself. One way must surely be when they come in the manner in which they come to me, as representatives of the collective consciousness of their species, and so totally in contact with their higher selves, that they are able to access great knowing and wisdom. This of course can then be passed on to us, just as it is in some of the messages that I have included in this book. The elephants here on Earth in physical form, by the means of their presence, give us the opportunity to study them and learn from what we see. I feel sure that where their physical presence is concerned, there must be many subtle ways in which they work, but it does not come within my knowledge to explain it any more than that.

The Flowering Tree Ceremony in Africa

It was the first "free" morning that we had had since the start of our riding safari. It was a beautiful camp situated beside the Mara River. Some people just wanted to spend the time sleeping, others were busy with their cameras, and a few of us were doing things together with Linda, until finally the mid-day heat became too intense, and we decided to take a rest before lunch.

Part of the entertainment that we indulged in was the flowering tree ceremony, as described in my first chapter about trees. I have stated therein, that if you practise it, gradually the answers tend to get longer. This is how it was for me on my second attempt, nearly a whole year later. I call it channelling (for oneself) with the help of a tree.

"Who am I?"

I am spirit, a free spirit. In this moment I dwell in human clothing. My attachment to this human life form is temporary. It is transient, a fleeting experience.

"Where did I come from?"

I come from the heart of the Great Spirit. I have reached out to the extremities of his being to experience all that is.

"Where am I going?"
Far away to a distant star,
Beyond the moon and sun,
For I can freely travel there
When duties here are done.

"What am I doing?"

Learning, bringing understanding to humanity. Reminding them of things long forgotten. I too am slowly remembering, as I learn to submerge my spirit into the depthless sea of knowing; as I seek out a pathway, as I search for new ways of being, as I strive to awaken and understand my power, as I rejoice in its extensiveness, and look for ways of bringing others with me to share this new found joy. It feels very early yet. It is as a springtime.

(Continued beside a second tree. I thought that I had finished, but when I saw that nobody else had, I decided to do some more while I was waiting. I selected another tree, and received the following.)

"I am a teacher who is learning. Still hampered by personality, I am looking for the strength to bring more light into my being. As I cast the walls around me aside, (there is still much work to do here) I seek connection with all life, particularly here on the Earth. This last point is hard for me at times, as Earth has in so many past lives been as a prison for me in my unknowing. It takes all my courage to wholeheartedly seek to re-connect with it. The soul of the planet needs our love and care. Man is the most influential creature on the planet. Just as the potential for joy here is great, so is our responsibility to cherish and care for all that is around us."

I found that the above seemed to put me in touch with where I was spiritually at that particular time. A small group of us had all done this, and listening to each others results was fascinating, especially as some had never tried it before, but were still successful.

Instructions For Me

After our time in Mombassa, where I had enormously enjoyed the snorkelling about three quarters of an hour further along the coast line, we took a train back to Nairobi. I was not sitting there comfortably relaxed, but perched on the edge of my seat, trying to make sure that neither the backs of my thighs nor the skin on my back were subjected to any pressure, for I was very sun-burnt. When I was back in England, I met a colleague who told me, "Oh, for snorkelling one wears an old T-shirt to protect one's back, because it is in the water that the sun can really burn you." If only I had known. On the boat I had been really careful covering up any exposed skin, but I thought that I could survive a short spell in the water, as I already had a slight tan from the summer. I am including this little tale in the hopes of sparing someone else going through similar agony afterwards. I was lucky that I did not get sunstroke. When I returned to England's cooler climate, I was quick to acquire chilblains on top of the burns on my thighs, which made it all very slow to heal up.

Back to my story. Sitting perched precariously on the edge of my train seat, I saw three elephants arriving, one of them quite big, but the other two standing one on either side of it, and a little further back were smaller. As they stood there with the trees around them, they started talking about the team work again. The two smaller ones were now far enough forward for the trunks of all three to become thoroughly intertwined and knotted. They seemed to be indicating working very closely together.

Next, I saw the pages of a book of short chapters with the first letter of each beautifully illuminated. "It must be illustrated", I heard the elephants say, and realised that they were referring to this book.

Lastly, I found myself above the largest elephant, and being brought face downwards until with my body horizontal, I was close enough for my energy centres and consciousness to blend with those of the elephant. This was the second time that this strange procedure had taken place.

When I considered the team work that they referred to, and the fact that there were three elephants, and that they showed themselves so closely connected with their trunks, I felt that they were trying to tell me that three people should be involved with the production of this book. Well, there would be me, and then very clearly Linda, although I did not realise that at the time, but have discovered it since, as she has helped me so much with advice on how to write it. (I will tell more of that later.) So who could the third person be? I wondered if it might be an illustrator, but the answer was not to come to me for another thirteen months, so I will tell of that when I get that far.

So the Africa trip was nearly over. There is one last point of interest to make. In the chapter headed "Africa or Not?", I described how there were five or six angels, who said that they would be with me throughout the trip. When I wondered what sort of angels they were, or even if they were really angels, they told me that they were stewards of the Earth. Now when I was riding across the African plains, and just after the communication with the Spirit of Africa, I saw five or six rays of soft gold light reaching down to the earth. "We are stewards of the earth", they told me. I suppose that this was the confirmation that they had kept their word, and had been with me for every step of the way.

Chapter 19

Crystal Meditation in the Forest

t was not very long after my return from Africa, that I was to be found riding my beautiful horse in the forest through the pine trees. Although it was December, the weather was mild and peaceful, and the horse (referred to as "Wilderness" later in the book) was walking quietly and willingly. My attention began to drift. Much as I enjoyed the beauty of the trees and my horse, I felt sad. Life in Africa had been so eventful, and now back in England, I felt as though I had lost whatever progress I had made and pleasant as life was, I relapsed into my usual bad habit of wishing that I was somewhere else. When I found that this drift of my attention was leading me straight into a meditation, I welcomed it.

I saw a tunnel filled with white-blue light, and started to travel down it. The far end appeared to be blocked by a sheet of almost solid golden light, as though the realms beyond were forbidden. Determined to break free from my limitations, so that I could enjoy the freedom of exploring further, I flung my total consciousness at the sheet of gold, and broke through it. On the other side was a whole new world. I felt overwhelmed by the peace and tranquillity and light there. I found that I had brought with me negative vibrations of anxiety and stress, and it felt as though all the darkness from my environment was still attached to me as well.

Such things were so out of place here, that I felt like some kind of mistake who should never really have arrived there at all. "I will have to change my vibrations so that I fit in better here", I said to myself. At a loss as to how to tackle this, I looked around for help. Almost immediately, I saw a beautiful angel-like being with a radiance of pure white light standing beside me. The angel drew closer, enveloping me in its light, and reached out to touch me. The unwanted negative vibrations vanished. I can only suppose that they had been transmuted into light. There were quite a few other people standing about, mostly completely absorbed in whatever they were doing. I didn't think that they had physical bodies anymore. They seemed to fit in with this beautiful place of light very well. I made no connection to them, for there were other things for me to do. My attention was suddenly taken by something that I had hitherto not noticed. It appeared to be an enormous beautifully clear skyblue quartz crystal. It stood roughly four or five feet tall. The angel took me over to it. I entered into the very centre of the crystal.

As my energy centres became perfectly aligned with the heart of the crystal, I began to feel it pulsating within me. At each pulsation, I felt my own chakra energy system being stretched and extended outwards, and then released again. I saw this blue-white light or energy form of the crystal working away inside me. I was in the crystal, and the crystal was in me. At last I stepped outside again, and as I looked around myself, I saw that there were other crystals just as large dotted about on the landscape, but these others were all pure white. All of them were many sided, and every side had many facets on it. They may have been six-sided. This was truly a healing place, and a place for expansion. I thanked the angel, and returned to my horse and the pine trees. It had been a beautiful journey. As I continued riding through the trees, I observed that I did not feel the same as before. There was something inside me which felt as though it had been altered, and become more expansive. This was such a powerful experience, that I could not help wondering how large a part the energy field of my horse had played in this. Perhaps that had nothing to do with it, but as Wilderness is a powerful animal both physically and mentally, I think he may have provided a little energy.

Chapter 20

The Desert

fter December 1989, months seemed to go by with almost nothing from the animals. Sometimes I saw them around, but they were simply there, and I would find nothing to write down. After all, "I saw a tiger. It stayed for thirty seconds. Then it left", is hardly a worthwhile story; so such little happenings, which were infrequent over this period never reached paper. The infrequency of anything in my spiritual life during this time made it seem as though I was crossing a desert. Any little animal-comings were like tiny oases, like little reminders that there was something beyond this physical reality with which we are all so familiar. The bareness of this period, therefore, is my reason for heading this chapter "The Desert". I must admit that I did not go out of my way to meditate very much, but then I knew that if the animals or anyone else really wanted to reach me, that they would be able to, regardless of whether or not I was meditating. After all, my Uncle Edward had finally made it, and so had they in the past.

By 19th. April, I felt that I had just enough information to justify writing it down, a little oasis, you could say.

It seemed that there was not only a council of animals, but also a council of elephants. I concluded this, because they kept on appearing in numbers together. For several days in a row, I was aware of them milling about round me. On one occasion, they also had a rhinoceros with them, who walked up to me and stood facing me head on, so that I had a first class view of his magnificent ivory tusk. I only saw the big one at the front, because the little one was hidden behind it. He reminded me of a rich person unable to conceal his wealth, living in the constant fear of attack from greedy thieves. The elephants of this particular group were expressing the same grievance. They walked about uneasily in the trees, some of them displaying spectacular ivory, and others just empty holes where tusks had once been. The more that I looked, the more elephants I could see. "What are they worrying about?", I asked myself. "They seem to be really thick among the trees." Suddenly I realised that that was what they were worried about. They were too thick among the trees. That is to say, there were no longer enough trees for the elephants. Their environment is threatened and diminishing, and they need more land with trees on it, both for food and shelter, or shade from the sun. Leading up to this last part, they had tried appearing to me just after I had got into bed. Out of the blue, they would appear standing in a semicircle round me, saying nothing, but just looking or gazing intently at me.

On another occasion during this period, I was meditating, and just about to start healing the planet, when I realised that I was sitting in water, part of the ocean, I suppose. Swimming towards me, I saw a beautiful seal. Its fur was quite light coloured under its tummy, but darker over its back. It came so close that its soft pale under-side brushed lightly against mine. It felt really wonderful, like the most blissful possible form of massage. It continued to swim to and fro, each time brushing itself against my body in passing, and then with its nose, touching and nuzzling me against the back of my neck before it left.

Before the seal had completely disappeared from sight, and while I was still sitting in the depth of the ocean, a badger arrived, complete with its own little patch of dry land. It remained a little distance away from me, and then returned to wherever it came from. Both of these animals are threatened by the activities of mankind, but apart from that, I could not find any reason for their coming.

June arrived, and I felt that I was still in the desert. After all, the above was all that I had had since December. Although I had received no further instructions for the book from the animals, I began to wonder if their silence was an indication that their communications were finished, and that it was time to put together those that I had, and get them published. The elephants had always seemed to be in a hurry to have word put round, whatever the other animals might feel.

In spite of my dislike of type-writers, my logic told me that I stood a better chance of persuading a publisher to read what I had written if it did not entail struggling to read through pages of hard-to-read scrawly hand-writing. Therefore I moved some of the dust off a typewriter that I had never mastered using properly many years ago, and having rediscovered the ancient text book which showed me where to put my fingers on its keys, I endeavoured to type out this book. It was a very laborious process. My handwriting had always been slower than most people's, but my typing took much much longer. Luckily at that time, the book was much much shorter, and therefore I was able to complete the work in time to take a copy of it to Germany at the end of June to show Linda T.-J., who knew of a publisher in the States. I should have known when I drew a tarot card called "disappointment", that things were not going to go as I hoped they would. Linda took the script back to the States with her, and after having shown it to a publisher, gave me their unanimous opinion, namely that it was just a skeleton for a book.

In spite of the helpful comments and advice that were given to me so freely, I still felt heart-broken that my work of art was unacceptable in the way in which I had presented it. I felt that it was my mission to get the information out into the World somehow, otherwise I was letting the animals down. The most important clue that Linda gave me for achieving this, was when she told me how she and the publisher had both decided that I should wait until I was further down my spiritual pathway. As I have already mentioned, I am a "Let's have it done by yesterday." person, and further down the pathway sounded like at least three or four years, which to me was an eternity. How could I hurry this up? If I had to wait until I automatically arrived there, it would mean not weeks, but several years of living on the planet with no real purpose for being here. I already knew how bad that felt, so I carried out the only alternative that I could think of, which was to travel down the intended pathway faster. There were things in my personality that were serious blocks to any hope of my being able to achieve a successful book, and my only hope of altering this in a sufficiently drastic fashion would be with intensive help from someone on a one-to-one basis.

Group work is wonderful. I had done plenty of that, and will do more. Nonetheless this time I needed not an express train, but a jumbo jet. So where would my intuition lead me to find the answer? I had long ago learnt that intuitive decisions in these situations are vital, as they are the best, as one is allowing one's own higher-self to play a part, and it is far far wiser than any amount of intellectual brain power will ever be. It led me to Chris Griscom, and what a brilliant move that turned out to be. The earliest that I could arrange it was in October, and although between June and then I kept on getting the occasional little messages from the animal kingdom; as far as any real attempt to rewrite my book was concerned, I was very conscious of something that told me to wait. I knew that I would reach the end of the desert in October, and with this knowledge, I no longer felt lost in the desert. It had become a much friendlier place to be in.

Chapter 21

Talking to Horses

spent a week in Reken, Germany, just north of Dusseldorf in order to participate in one of Linda T.-J.'S week-long trainings. This was when I gave her a copy of the script to take home to the States, as I have already mentioned, but that was not all that happened there.

A lady who was not participating in Linda's training came by invitation one evening to lead a meditation which was designed to help people have a two way communication with a horse. She organised it like a led meditation in which one could connect with the spirit of a horse (in my case my own horse) no matter how many miles away its body might be at the time.

Some of the while I was able to allow myself to be led, and at other times the action itself seemed to take over, and I would no longer be aware of the voice leading us.

Sitting under a tree, I watched my horse approaching. We were asked to ask whatever horse came what its name was, so I did, and the name "Wilderness" is what I heard. Now I had never called my horse by that name, but as the dictionary definition of 'wilderness' is 'desert', perhaps the name had more to do with what I was going through than the horse. I will call him Wilderness for the moment anyhow. When I started to look at my relationship with him, I was shown a pair of human hands with the fingers tightly interlocked. I had no idea before that I was so closely connected with him, although I did suspect that it was something beyond the usual amount. Next I saw Wilderness standing still on the left hand side of the picture, and there was a sturdy rope swinging towards me. There was also a river, and the purpose of the rope must surely be so that I could get hold of it, and then swing myself across the river to the far bank. I took hold of the rope, and tried to do this. No matter how hard I tried, at the end of each attempt, I always found myself instantly back where I had started, and saw the rope being offered to me yet again. "I must be missing some vital point here", I thought to myself, and reacted by trying to look more deeply at the benefits that my horse was bringing me in life.

The most salient point was surely that through his being there for my use, I was being given the opportunity to allow someone else to help me with the work and training that he and I carry out together. This is because I wish to do well in competitions with him, and dressage is not an easy thing for even the top riders to excel in, unless they allow someone to help them, for there is so much that can be achieved best with the aid of a second person. I was finding this a hard lesson, as I am always so full of my own ideas. I had, however, been giving someone the chance to help me, and only with great difficulty suppressing some of my own judgements, but it had rewarded me with some first prizes. In other words, thanks to these opportunities with my horse, I was learning to take advice.

Most people can ask for advice, but it is a lesser number who can follow it. It was also enabling me to develop the quality of being able to trust another person, as well as self-control, concentration, and the feminine attribute of allowing oneself to be controlled by something or someone external to oneself. The red rosettes and success were of little importance. It was the lessons learnt on the road to these successes that counted. What was there in all this for the horse? It was the opportunity for close interaction with human beings, the development of his personality, and the discovery for him of how many amazing things he could learn to do with a human partner. Wilderness was learning to go beyond what he had previously considered his limitations.

From the moment that I really grasped the significance of all this, I was able to swing over the river, after which both river and rope disappeared. Wilderness, delighted with my progress, turned on his heels, and galloped off up the hill, which was not very steep, but a slope, nonetheless, that the two of us were to negotiate together.

Although I had not realised quite how closely our destinations were linked before this meditation, I did know a little bit about it, which I now propose to share.

I had had Wilderness for about four months. Often when I rode him, it would be either a 'serious' dressage training in a confined area, or else practice over fences for which he had endless enthusiasm. On other days I would ride him out in the country which gave both of us a change, and could be both fun and relaxing. It was on such a day, that I kept on forgetting that it was *Wilderness who I was riding, and instead thinking that it* was actually a previous favourite horse of mine who died in 1979, (the horse 'Desert' already referred to in the introduction). Then I would jerk myself back to what I considered to be reality, and remind myself that I was sitting on Wilderness. Admittedly, the two horses were quite similar in some ways. Both had more than the average amount of beauty, both had a long sweeping stride, were fairly narrow and comfortable to sit on, and both of them had that well-bred look about them that thoroughbreds or near thoroughbreds characteristically show. Neither was good for going to sleep on, as both had too much spirit. Both were highly intelligent. I had really adored the other horse who had stayed with me for twelve years, and having seen him several times just *after his death, I started to wonder if this could be a return visit.* I had not thought of him for ages, but felt those familiar vibrations in the body of this six year old that I was now riding in his place. For the purposes of this book, I have chosen to call this previous horse Desert, because the meaning of 'desert' is so close to the meaning of 'wilderness', and also Desert was half arab, which makes the name Desert very appropriate for him.

Later in the year I met a friend who had also picked up a connection between the two horses, although I had told her none of my own feelings about it. Her theory was that Desert had returned as a spiritual guide for Wilderness. To begin with I accepted her idea, but I knew that she did not believe in reincarnation for anybody, and it was still puzzling me that whenever either of these two visited me in my dreams, they shared the same identity. Only the colour would vary, changing from what it was to what it is, or vice versa. Then I realised that Wilderness had been born within a year of Desert dying. Slowly I reached the realisation that they were both the same horse. The love link had been very strong, and Desert had found his way back to me.

Then I remembered what it had been like when someone had first told me that Wilderness was for sale. Although I had been thinking that it would be better not to buy a horse just yet, as I had a nice little jumping mare, whom I wanted to take to a few more shows before parting with her, and in spite of telling my informer that "Yes, I will try and find out if any of my clients would like to buy that horse of your sister's", inside I already knew that I felt a strong urge to buy it for myself. I had not even seen it, and yet without any first hand impressions of it, I felt that I had to get it. After seeing him, and experiencing that possessive feeling of "this is my horse", I went through the usual formality of calling the veterinary surgeon to see if his health was good enough to warrant purchase, but it was almost as though the vet. could have told me that Wilderness was going to die tomorrow, and I would still have bought him.

I remembered how after Desert's death, he had returned to me during the night some three weeks later, and showed me how he could now manage some of the difficult dressage movements which I had failed to teach him during his lifetime, due to failing health on his part, and lack of skill on mine. As Wilderness, he returned as a bolder stronger model. Within a few years we were able to achieve some of the things (especially jumping) that I had never managed with him before. It was as though we were completing some unfinished business together. My suspicions were confirmed when I read a book in which the author describes how he and his wife used to astral travel together at night. On their return to the bedroom one night, they noticed the astral body of a deceased cat, a previous favourite of theirs. Its fluffy light form floated towards the wife, and then the husband noticed that there was a silver cord coming from it, which he was able to trace down through the darkness to one of their newly acquired kittens downstairs. Clearly the much loved cat had reincarnated, and found its way back to them. For me, this was the final piece of evidence that I needed to accept that animals do reincarnate, and that sometimes the domesticated ones like to return to their original owners. My two horses are one.

It is my intention that the inclusion of the above account will provide comfort for anyone who reads it having lost a favourite animal of any kind through death; and that they will know that death is not the end for animals any more than it is for us. It may not even be the end of the friendship, as a reunion can take place in the night, or after the death of both parties, or even during this lifetime if the animal chooses to reincarnate, and return to the owner in a brand new physical body.

The Oatcake Story

I never wrote this down when it happened. I just thought, "Oh yes, the horse was saying something to me, which only relates to me, and therefore nobody else needs to hear about it." Then, as I was writing a letter to Linda T.-J., I suddenly felt moved to recount the story to her. Perhaps it would help someone else who has made similar efforts to know how grateful the animals are when we try to understand them. Linda certainly thought so, as I discovered when she answered my letter. Although it was a month or two ago, the main points are still clear in my memory.

First of all, I wish to define an oatcake. It was not just any old oatcake that I will be referring to, but a Staffordshire oatcake. These are made mostly from oatmeal, and are about eight inches across. They are soft and flexible like an English pancake. Therefore one can put one's favourite filling in the middle, be it sweet or savoury, and roll them up. When I worked in Staffordshire, I grew particularly fond of these, and also rather fat. I had never seen them in any other part of the country, although they are available more widely now. I remember one little shop where they made nothing else, and you could watch them being cooked, and buy them really fresh. They are a speciality of the Potteries, as this area is called, where Wedgewood china and other pottery is made.

I was meditating at home, when a fairly small woolly-looking grey pony came to see me. He wore a red nylon headcollar, which suggested to me that he must be representing all horses kept by humans, or more or less that. He stood before me, and I noticed that he had a Staffordshire oatcake which he held in his mouth. This choice morsel of food was dropped at my feet like an offering. I knew that horses liked oats, but who told them that I liked oatcakes I wonder? This little gift was being presented to me as an acknowledgement of my efforts to understand his kind. "We want to thank you", he said. I knew that I had tried particularly hard recently to understand the minds of the horses with whom I was working. I had really tried to reach out to them. Evidently this had not passed un-noticed. Unfortunately, I could not eat the oatcake, because it only existed on a non-physical dimension, but I really understood what people mean when they use the expression "It's the thought that counts". I felt deeply moved by this unexpected acknowledgement. As I sat there, tears came to my eyes, and the pony left.

I have thought since of how many other people would have similar experiences, if they were psychic enough to receive them. That is why this needs to be shared.

Chapter 22

The Last Lap of My Journey Through the Desert

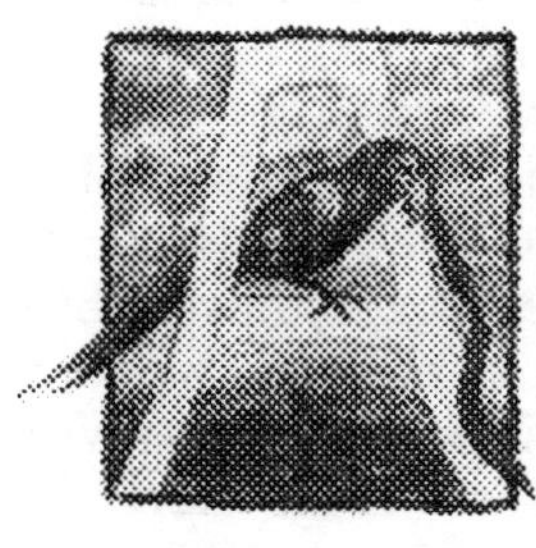

nimal appearances were fairly rare during this time, but they did come about once a month. In July it was the two elephants on top of a hill on Lanzerote explaining what had been meant by pressure points, as I have already described earlier on in this book. In August, it was a parrot.

I was at home, and piece by piece a bird started to come into view. It had colours of strong red, greens, a little yellow, and slightly blueish legs. In the course of the following conversation the colours varied a bit, changing to greener shades, which suggested to me that this bird represented not just one species of parrot, but a whole section of the Earth's birds. As the first red feathers came into view around the head with a yellow beak, and then the red feathers in the tail, a truly splendid bird took form. "I am a parrot", it repeated at least three times just to make sure that I got the message. "Men copy too. They copy as well." I did not understand the significance of that straight away, so I continued watching and listening. Round one of its legs was a little metal ring. "I am a tame parrot", it continued. Next it took a long thin red silk scarf, wrapped it around my neck, and seemed to want to strangle me with it. "Why are you doing this?", I asked. "Men treat us as such silly birds that I could happily strangle them", came the reply. "We sit here pecking away at millet in small cages. Men regard us as stupid, because when we speak their language, we simply copy what we have heard. Our language is seldom understood by them. So often when we live in captivity, our intelligence remains underdeveloped, for we lack the opportunity in a small cage to try things out, and learn in any way that might help us to reach our natural potential as birds. We need space to move about and stretch our wings, if we are to live so close to mankind in captivity. Not only that, but physical contact with our keepers would also help to make the relationship more mutually beneficial. If they would sometimes touch us, or stroke us gently with their hands, not to frighten us, but often enough for us to be able to cast fear aside, and enjoy the experience. We need as many different and varied opportunities as ingenuity can conjure up to interrelate with them, so that they can know us as personalities. This would be so helpful both to bird and man."

When I thought about it, I realised that it is tradition to think of birds as stupid, but then we judge them by our own standards, and overlook some of the amazing qualities that they have, which any good naturalist could tell you about. Instead, we have expressions like 'bird-brained' for silly people who forget easily, or seem to have very small brains, and then there is the expression 'parrot fashion'. We were often told at school, "Don't just learn it parrot fashion", implying that we should seek the deeper meaning of things beyond the words, rather than merely being able to recite them.

In September, there came two messages fairly close together, but quite different from each other. The first one concerned a seal. Towards the end of my meditation, I saw one on the beach. It was sitting up looking at me with big brown wide open eyes. It did not move, and communicated telepathically with me.

"With so much history behind us, we approach you now to make you aware of part of our purpose and role in creation here on Earth. We are a link in a chain. This refers to our consciousness, not to our biological aspects, although they also are of worth in nature's balance on another level. On the level of consciousness, we are as a link between mankind and those who dwell on the land, and the deep sea animals, and most especially the big evolved fishes, such as whales and dolphins. As you see, we spend much time on the shore fulfiling this function."

The second message, which followed soon afterwards, came from a hen. She stood before me in her beautiful golden brown plumage. She was facing me, and peered at me first with one eye, and then the other. She had her own kind of dignity, and was proud to be a hen. She showed me a hen in a very small cage, and began to speak of battery hens, and overcrowding. "But kept like this", she explained, "nature goes berserk".

I was reminded of the stories I had heard, not only of hens pecking one another badly, but also of them actually murdering each other in big numbers, where they had been kept in overcrowded conditions, as though they had all gone crazy. This is just part of the chaos and misery wrought by mankind. The hen wanted me to understand and make it known that only when these birds are properly looked after, and kept in humane conditions can they be how the Creator intended.

October 17th. produced my final animal communication before I went to Switzerland to join Chris Griscom's workshop. The last, but not the least, as I consider it quite deep and powerful in its implications.

I found myself sitting in a clearing in a wood. I was cross-legged on the grass. The colours around me were mostly shades of soft green, and I experienced an overwhelming sense of peace. The clearing was circular, and surrounded by tall mature trees. Although I was aware of colours, when I looked up, I saw that there was a night sky with a full moon, the light of which was shining down powerfully into the clearing, and even enabling me to see a little way into the trees. The scene was set, and I began to feel a change taking place in the vibrations present. Looking round, I saw the animals starting to gather at the edge of the trees. It was the complete Council of Animals.

When I wondered if they were really all there, the white rabbit became particularly active, as though he were trying to reassure me through his presence that all of the others were also there. I kept seeing his long white ears with their pink insides, and two of his top front teeth visible resting just over his bottom lip. He was to make the first move, which was most surprising to me. He blew up a bright blue balloon, and then as he released it, it drifted up into the sky. Then the other animals followed suit, but each released a balloon of a different colour. The atmosphere felt like magic now. I watched what was going on spellbound. I sensed the excitement and the expectancy of something coming, the arrival of which, they were already beginning to celebrate. I could see leopard, tiger, elephant, camel, etc. moving restlessly round the circle through the trees. I could see little shining particles of magic in the air. I mean that the atmosphere itself was sparkling. This was a new phenomenon for me. "What is this all about?", I asked. They showed me a picture of myself kneeling on the ground in the middle of the circle thrusting my head forwards with my neck very obvious. "It is time for you to stick your neck out more", one of them said. I understood from this that a time was shortly coming, when it was intended that I show more of my true nature to the world, and speak more openly of things lying hidden in my heart. (This turned out to be true a week later with Chris Griscom.)

Without any conscious decision on my part, I found myself getting up and starting to leave the clearing by a path that had just opened up through the trees. As I looked down it, I saw light at the other end of it, a very beautiful light with rainbow colours rippling through it, and a soft fluorescent quality with vibrations of joy. Once more I experienced the animals walking through the trees on either side of me. I was holding hands with two of them, and although I do not know which animals they were, it never entered my mind that it should be strange that they had hands.

I wondered why I should be walking with the animals. They read my thoughts and replied, "Because you are one of us". "Could they mean that I was really an animal, and not a human being at all?", I queried to myself. "We are all the same. We all share the same essence. Do not try to see yourself as something different. We are fellow travellers going in the same direction. We are here to help one another along the pathway. Recognise this. As we see the animal in you, you must see that in us which exists in you also. It is time for the separation that man has put there to cease. It is time for him to awaken, and return to the fold. In fact you never left the fold. Just your consciousness of it was lost. Do not be deceived either by our physical forms or your own. Know that beyond these, we are as one, all part of the same creative energy."

At this point the vision faded. All that was left was a parrot in a tree saying, "Write it down! Write it down!". So I did.

Chapter 23
Switzerland

he purpose of my Swiss visit was to work with Chris Griscom and the Light Institute. My interest in Chris and her work had not been seriously triggered until 1988, when I was in Germany on one of Linda T.-J.s trainings, and Linda insisted on lending me what she told me was a really wonderful book. This book, it turned out, was called “Time is an Illusion” by Chris Griscom. I was so impressed with it, that not long afterwards, I ordered myself a second book of hers called “Ecstasy is a New Frequency”. By the time I had finished reading both of these, I had made the decision that one day when the time was right, I would really like to meet this woman.

At this point it was her philosophy that attracted me, for I knew nothing about how the Light Institute functioned. Linda, on the other hand, not only knew Chris personally, but had had experience of the private sessions both from Chris, and then later after Chris had stopped doing them herself, from one of the well trained facilitators, who was part of the Light Institute team of people carrying out Chris's work under her direction. In some respects, what they were doing was similar to the past life therapy work that Rhea Powers had previously done, and still taught, but everyone works a little differently. Both methods are extremely effective, but different. Linda's occasional references to these powerful Light Institute sessions had gradually increased my curiosity.

When I was growing up, especially in my late teens, and before I had started earning a wage, so that I was still dependent on the small allowance that my parents provided me with for clothes and other expenses, I was often a little short of money. My mother had explained to me that they did this to me deliberately, because it was only by not having quite enough, that I would be able to learn the value of it. They did not want me hungry, or without the necessities, but they wanted me to learn to be very careful with it. The system worked. I have always been very nervous about spending my money. My mother's words "Remember that there will be no more when you have spent it!", were constantly echoing in my ears, and singing their way round my head. Therefore when the question came up of buying an air ticket to the States, and paying for my sessions, I felt really worried about spending the money. I had heard through some of my continental friends that sometimes Chris made trips to Europe. Perhaps Germany, I thought, and that would be relatively on the doorstep. Also there would be no jet lag to contend with. So I started making inquiries, and learnt that a small group was being organised in Weggis, Switzerland, where Chris and six or seven of her facilitators would be present to work with us. This meant that each of us would receive four private three hour sessions from one of her facilitators, with the opportunity afterwards to talk to Chris in small groups to ask questions about anything that had come up in the sessions.

Although I had had this desire to find out more about Chris and her work for some time, and there were several issues about which I was hoping to satisfy my curiosity; my strongest motivation was to get myself into a state where I could successfully get the animal communications out into the world. The workshop was called "Sense of Success", and seemed to be aimed more at business people than the likes of me. That, combined with the expenses, had very nearly frightened me away, but this insistent voice inside me said, "But you will spare yourself so much pain if you go". That was the deciding factor. Pain is something for which I had extremely low tolerance, and the avoidance of pain totally justified any expense, and everything else that I could think of.

I arrived a day early, because by staying over a Saturday night, I was able to reduce the cost of my airfare by more than half. Actually, it turned out to be a brilliant idea, as with everything being new to me there, I found that I was really exhausted by the time that I arrived, and I needed the extra twenty-four hours rest before we started.

Working on yourself is seldom like lying on a bed of roses. It is usually a mixture of good and bad experiences, but the bad ones can really take some facing up to, so I was a little apprehensive. The good things provide their share of trouble as well, as I find it difficult to believe them! Perhaps my general state of anxiety is the reason why the following meditation occurred spontaneously. It turned out to be very appropriate.

I saw the white rabbit, who I am beginning to know so well from the council of animals. He stood there like a way-shower at the beginning of a path that I was clearly intended to negotiate. Dark as it was, I knew that the path had been prepared for me. There was, however, just enough light for me to see the way. I was shown how I was going to walk it alone, and yet there would always be other beings not far away watching me. The support would be there, but I must find my own footing. Halfway along the path I saw a giraffe, which, although walking in the shadows, was tall enough to reach upwards with his long neck, and look out over the sunlit tops of the trees. From this relatively high vantage point, it was possible to see not only where he was, but also where he had come from, and where he was going, as well as all around. I was reminded, that if I chose to let myself merge into his beautiful body, then even from my position in the shadows, I could reach up, and gain a much broader perspective on life. Secondly, I must not forget when I find myself in the shade, that the shadows are only possible when the sun is shining elsewhere.

I think that this thoughtful gift of foresight would have comforted me far more, if I had not totally forgotten about it until I found it written out on a scrap of paper after I had arrived home!

Past life work is controversial at the best of times. First of all there are those who choose not to accept re-incarnation as a possibility, and therefore put forward countless alternative explanations for the apparent success of others to recall past lives. Then there are those who concede that maybe they have lived before, but there are two many dangers involved in the hypnotic process often used for it to be a good idea to find out about it. Others say that if you keep on being "regressed", then you are really living in the past instead of the present, and still others say that one life at a time is enough thank you, and that just coping with the present incarnation is as much as the mind can handle. (Incidently, the Light Institute prefers not to use the term "regression", on the grounds that all lives are taking place simultaneously. After all, time is an illusion.)

So why was I so keen on remembering? Well first of all, it is a very liberating process, as it releases blocks hidden deep in the subconscious mind that you would otherwise know nothing about. Once discovered you can do something about them to take away their power. Only then can you let the past go. Until then, undiscovered, the past holds onto you, and holds you back. To what extent must surely vary from person to person. Past life memories travel with you from lifetime to lifetime, and my own experience has shown me that they are like a millstone round the neck, which frustrates even the most enthusiastic endeavours to move forwards as a person. My higher self was craving a release. You are not your past lives any more than you are this one. I am sure of that.

All of these different people that you have experienced being, and the person who you think you are now, are not you. They are just a string of different identities that you identify with for a learning process, which is mostly what life on Earth is about. I find that it is when I forget, and start to think that I am one of these identities that I lose who and what I really am. For like everyone else, I am a part of the Source, or God, the Great White Spirit, call it what you will. When in my forgetfulness, I fall into the trap of thinking that I am one of these identities, Helena, for example, that is when I experience the isolation of separation from my source, which is God.

When you recognise that what you really are is a part of pure God energy, totally innocent, and worthy of freedom to be what you really are, then you owe it to yourself to do all in your power to realise that. How can you love your neighbour as yourself, if you do not first learn to love yourself? If you look out on life, and see that the people round you are really suffering, then in order to help them, the first step is learning to love yourself, and for me a large part of it involves finding out who I really am.

Most of us have made so many mistakes in our other lives, that we are now very wary of trying things. We become too full of fear. Hidden in the sub-conscious mind is the knowledge that "When I tried that last time six lives ago, I was thrown into prison, which was unfair, but as that is what happened, and prison was a bad experience, I will refrain from doing that again". That is the sort of pattern that might emerge, and sometimes both powerful and restricting are the vows that we make. This is not a book on re-incarnation therapy, because there are so many other people better equipped to write one of those than me, but there is one life that came up this time at Weggis, which seems to have produced the kind of breakthrough that I was searching for.

Very briefly, it was as follows. I was a teacher, and I taught many things of an esoteric nature. I wanted to be a good person, but lacked the necessary wisdom to feel I could achieve that. I had excellent clairvoyance, but instead of using it wisely, helping the people who were ready to be helped by it, I went round giving out advice from my visions to those who had no interest in such things whatsoever. I meddled, or tried to meddle in other people's lives in this way. Not everyone wants to be corrected, and most people deeply resented my interference. Also it never occurred to me to look and see what my own errors in life were. I did not want to find out in case I did not like what I discovered. It was in this way that I failed to foresee how one day, with their patience at an end, two men would come, take me by force, and throw me into prison. It was customary for witches to be burned, and that is what happened to me. I still failed to see my own mistakes, and felt very bitter and angry about the lack of recognition that my talents had received. I had genuinely wanted to help humanity, and they had rewarded me with a death of shame. I vowed with all the strength that I possessed, that "I will never again under any circumstances ever do anything to help humanity".

Although I knew that in this life, I had never been what I would call a "people-person", I thought this quite natural in my case after the rejection that I had felt as a child, as well as the various gruesome events and suffering that I had undergone in other lives at the hands of humanity; although my approach to people had altered considerably after working on such things in Rhea Powers' workshops. Uncovering this vow, and receiving help from someone in seeing how I had brought my violent death upon myself through the injudicious use of my psychic gifts gave me an enormous increase in courage to use my gifts for others in this lifetime, but only for those who wish to benefit from them, rather than those who I think ought to be listening to what I have to share. It had really been a lesson in remembering that you can only teach someone when the pupil is ready to learn, and that people will only learn from you if you are living your own truth.

At the time of my session, I had no idea what a gift the release of this vow about not helping humanity would turn out to be. Then it was just another rather tough lesson to learn, just another chapter of my shady past unearthed. The changes that it had wrought were only brought home to me after my return to England, when I started writing up an account about mermaids, which I will tell more about shortly. Instead of writing in my usual style, whereby everything unnecessary concerning myself is omitted, I found that I was automatically setting the scene, putting down where I was, why, and what I was doing there, and trying to fill in everything that could possibly be of interest to anyone who chose to read it.

The whole thing was so much more open and informative. Much of the secrecy was gone. It made me start to think about Linda's advice about what was wrong with the original script. She had told me that I needed a ghost writer to set the scene for me, so that readers would be able to follow how these things had come about. She had explained that I needed more material, and that in spite of what was there, I needed to put a lot about myself. That had really horrified me. I thought that it was just fear of exposure or ridicule that was stopping me, but after Weggis, I saw that there was something else. If I were to put in things about my own struggle, and how I had been helped, and share what I had learnt, then I would really be doing something to help humanity, but hidden in my subconscious mind was this vow that I would never ever do that again. No wonder that I did not want to share myself. I looked again at the script. It read like a shopping list. There was nothing to connect it all together. How on earth could I make it into a readable story?

The answer came to me when I was lying relaxing in the bath. I saw a golden chain, in which the missing link was just being added, and a voice said, "The missing link is you". So that was it! Linda had said months ago, that the animals wanted me to put more about me, but I simply could not bring myself to do it. As far as publishing what the animals had to say was concerned, that was quite acceptable. I really did want to help them, as well as the rest of nature, and the planet. I knew that it was necessary to educate mankind, as otherwise the planet, the animals, and all of nature would continue to suffer. Mankind, as the most destructive creature on the planet, badly needed a raising and expansion of awareness and consciousness. I could see that, but let the animals do it I thought. If they wanted to channel their help to humanity through me, then I would willingly be their scribe, and that was fine, as I really did want a purpose for being here.

Now it was different. Everything seemed to have changed. I was ready for a much more personal commitment. I was certain that my number one commitment in life at this moment was to start re-writing the book. The channellings so carefully recorded would remain unaltered, but there was a lot of explaining to do, and as I set about a fuller introduction, the words seemed to come tumbling out of the typewriter. I realised how important it was for others to realise that I was not some kind of incarnated angel, but someone so human, that I could suffer and make mistakes in abundance. I wanted it to be known how much help I had needed and received from outside myself, and that now I am only just beginning. It is my wish that from my story others will gain hope, and that they will not need to make quite as many mistakes as I have, but will be able to benefit by learning from some of mine.

I want everyone to know that it does not matter how low one has let oneself sink, there is always a road back up. Choose to climb it, and happiness can become ones own. This road is known as the Spiritual Pathway. It can be steep and rough going, but the light gets brighter the higher one climbs, and the greater the struggle, the greater the rewards. Pain may not end, but there is never more than one can cope with. Although I still have a very long way to travel, I do not regret one step that I have taken.

Chapter 24
Mermaids in Switzerland

s so often is the case, something will happen which then triggers off something else. In this case, it was to do with mermaids. The 'something' was a conversation with Chris Griscom during one of our question and answer times. The idea that I should ask her about mermaids popped up in my mind so suddenly, that I never had time to think about how out of place this question was going to sound in a workshop aimed at the business world. So I did not ask "What should I do in order to gain more clients, and become richer or better known?", which would have been a very suitable question. Instead some inner urging prompted me so forcefully, and so suddenly to ask, "Could you possibly say a word or two about mermaids?", that the question was out before I had time to think about it. I may be wrong, but I thought that Chris looked a little surprised. Perhaps she was just pausing to think about it before answering. I sat there wondering if she would take me seriously or not, but serious I definitely was.

Linda was the only person to whom I had dared to mention mermaids before, so when Chris waited a moment or two before giving a reply, I was more than a little worried. She spoke first of some of the beings from the time of Atlantis, the lost continent that disappeared into the Pacific Ocean. These beings had been half man and half animal, but mermaids, she continued were something quite different. There followed a pause during which she looked round at me. I did not know for what reason, but I thought that perhaps she was looking in case I was sceptical, or just asking from a mild curiosity, and that really I did not have any genuine interest in such things. Anxious to reassure her that none of that was the case, and that this unusual question was critically important to me, for I knew of few people on Earth who were suitable for such a question, not to mention the reassurance so badly needed that my own experiences were genuine, I added that the reason led me to ask the question was that I had been visited by mermaids on two separate occasions. Chris told me that the ability to communicate with other species was such a gift with so much obvious sincerity, that I knew I had really directed this question at exactly the right person. Deeply grateful for this recognition of the validity of my mermaid communications, and also of the desirability of them, I became much more open to receiving any further communications that they might choose to make.

Later that evening in my hotel room, I was lying on my bed reading a book about colour and the aura, when I became aware that I had company. A little to my left I saw a mermaid. Actually, I could not see the whole of her, because there was so much light radiating out from her solar plexus, that the central part of her body was hidden from view. She was sitting out of the water on a rock. It was night time, and I could see the ocean stretching away behind her, with rocks looming up out of it here and there, and the moonlight shining on the water. I looked straight at her, and saw that she was now sending me a beam of very bright high intensity light, although I only discovered that that was what it was, when Chris told me later. It seemed to enter right into my body, and I felt afraid of it. I had never experienced anything like this before.

When light shines out from a torch, it is strong and powerful where it leaves the torch, but then it broadens out into a much more diffuse light covering a wider area, the further away it gets from the torch. This light from the mermaid was different. Instead of being round at the base, it was square. It did not broaden out as it travelled, but had the same diameter where it entered my body as it had had where it left hers, and therefore none of its brightness or intensity was lost. Chris had told us earlier in the day, that one of the ways of coping with fear is to expand your aura. So I did that, and sent to her a diffuse white light. By now, she was sending me flashes of light, which I found fairly disconcerting. After a while that stopped, and I had another idea. I remembered how it was possible to use colours for communication. Therefore I asked the mermaid's higher-self what colour would she like me to send her. To my delight, she answered me.

Then there followed a short period in which we took it in turns to send each other colours. This all happened so fast that I could not remember who sent what to whom, or in what order the colours came. I do not remember any pink or red, but the last colour used was gold. It may have been the mermaid who sent that to me, but I am not certain. By this time I had become much more relaxed with her, in fact my fear had totally subsided, which gave me the presence of mind to ask, "What is this all about?". In reply, she showed me a very delicate and intricate gold bridge. I understood this to symbolise the bridging of consciousness between her reality and mine. She gave me the understanding that the different realms of consciousness needed to be brought together to increase their strength on the planet. It has something to do with holding this reality together. Then I noticed that I was looking at the whole picture through a gap in a wall, which had been the dividing line between her dimension and mine. The picture faded, and she vanished.

The following day, feeling a mixture of doubts and questions, I decided to talk to Chris about this. During the sessions, a number of us including me, had not only worked on clearing past lives, but also on clearing possessive energies. These can take many different forms. According to Chris, all of us tend to be possessed in some way or another, even if we are unaware of it, which we usually are. It can be possession by astral entities, or sometimes by thought forms prevalent in the atmosphere which attach themselves to the emotional body, and exert a strong influence over our thinking and behaviour. In order to be there, possessive energies will go to any length to disguise their presence with various cunning methods of deception. Therefore my question to Chris concerning the mermaid was, "Could she have been a disguised possessive entity, in which case I should send her away as soon as possible; or was she really a mermaid as she appeared to be, in which case I wanted to welcome her, and how could I tell the difference?". "After all," I thought to myself, "if some cunning astral being, wanting to be with me rather than where ever he or she should be, were to discover that although I sent most astral beings away, I am very fond of mermaids; then an excellent choice of disguise would be to appear as a mermaid".

Chris explained that possessive entities (or energies) were there because they wanted something from you. Whereas this mermaid was just a temporary visitor there for something else, and was very valid. The high intensity light that she sent me has very fast vibration, and can be quite scary, as it excites the shakti (pure divine energy) which travels up and down the spine. Also, instead of sending the white light straight at her, just radiating it out would have been better.

Now that I knew that the high intensity white light was something good, another of my fears had been dispelled.

Chapter 25

A Real Mixture of Things

y life after Weggis was unusually hectic, so it was quite a while before I was able to give my book a thought, or had time to meditate much, but by mid-November life was nearly back to normal, and I was getting a few visits from the animals again.

One of the most curious things that happened took place while I was dancing. It is a habit of mine, that often before I go to bed, I light a candle, draw the curtains to, put on what ever music I am in the mood for, and move to it. I either let my body do exactly what it wants to do, or else I try to let it express the music, so that I get the feeling that the music is expressing itself through my body, or a mixture of both of these. I find it a wonderful way to release any tension that I have, as well as to make the body feel really good, and the whole thing tends to still the mind. Best of all, I enjoy it.

On this particular night, I had not been doing this for more than about five minutes, when I noticed that there were a lot of little shining lights dotted about around my shoulders, and down my back. These were connected to one another by lines of light. They were like energy paths running around my body. I realised after a moment or two that these must be the meridians that are referred to by those who practise acupuncture, and the little lights were acupoints. I know that they exist all over the body, but I only saw them in the places that I have mentioned. Now what intrigued me most of all was seeing how the more that I moved, the brighter the lights shone out, and the more alive I began to feel. It was as though my body was waking up and coming to life. I only remained this tuned in for a minute or two, but the whole thing had been completely spontaneous. I would never have thought of looking for such things. Another point that I find so curious about it was that as far as I could tell, I remained totally in my body for the whole of it, and yet, when I saw these meridians, I was definitely watching myself as though I was standing behind me. I can not do this at will. It either happens, or it does not.

Still in November, as I was wandering round the house, in a clearing covered with good grass, and surrounded by trees, I saw a small herd of black and white cattle. They were just standing there looking at me. They had such appealing faces that they were irresistible. The picture faded, and I carried on with my tasks about the house. "Cows! That's unusual", I thought to myself, "Haven't had those before".

The next time they came, I was meditating. It was only a short visit, but this time they had something to communicate. They wanted to tell me of their concern about how domestic cattle were being treated. It was all very wrong. The things done to cattle are not moral. They were not complaining about being eaten as you might think on this occasion, but about the exploitation of nature that takes place in intensive farming with extensive use of steroids, anti-biotics, overcrowding in small areas, instead of a more natural life in a meadow, and all of the other inhumane things that go on. Abattoirs, it is fairly widely known, are often cruel through lack of sympathy and understanding for the animals, but there is so much that happens in between birth and reaching the slaughter house that is also very wrong and immoral. I would have given you all this in their exact words, only they did not use any. I received the concepts telepathically in a wordless communication, so I have had to use my own words for them.

Early December brought some sea turtles along. At first it was just one of them. It came towards me, and stopped in front of me. "I come from the sea", it said, "and we are being overlooked". I felt that this meant that their welfare and conservation were not getting enough attention. "Fishermen's nets are a hazard", it added. What fascinated me were the turtle's eyes. It was really looking at me in such a questioning way. When I saw a mother turtle with her family of babies behind her, I realised that I was being shown things in a symbolic way, as I am pretty sure that baby turtles do not follow their mothers like that. It made it easier for me to understand what she was talking about. It was the little baby turtles who were having to grow up in polluted water. It was poisoning them. We should look after the sea more.

(After note. In 1996, approximately eight years after I received this message, I discovered that there were turtles swimming around Hawaii suffering from some form of cancer thought to be caused by the pollution in the oceans.)

Chapter 26

Mermaids Again

ver this November-December period of 1990, from time to time I found the mermaids floating in and out of my consciousness. Sometimes they felt quite distant, so that I was not even sure if they were there or not. Other times it was clearer, or even very clear. I saw many different colours with them; that is their own colours seemed to vary, and included not just the blues and greens that I had previously associated with mermaids, but also the warm colours as well.

One evening at home, I saw one sitting on the rocks with the sun in the background, and in the sea around the rocks were many fishes jumping up out of the water just in front of her. Another time, I was being sent light again, but the experience was not as powerful as the first time. Another difference was the shape of the light. Instead of coming from something square-shaped, it came from a triangle.

During a more recent encounter, we seemed to be in the water on the bed of the ocean where there was much coral life around us. The mermaid was holding a beautiful crystal in her hands, and she invited me to step into it. Now I had been inside a crystal on another dimension before, which was when I was riding Wilderness through the pine trees, but that time some force outside myself had put me into it. I had no idea how it had happened, and therefore did not know how to repeat the experience. So there I was, sitting in front of her looking at the crystal in her hands, and wondering how to get inside it. "Try looking out of it from the inside", she advised me. I did, and in a flash, I found myself inside. It was a beautiful crystal, quite unlike the blue one that I had been in before. This one combined a sort of fluid quality with peace and tranquillity. Mostly it was colourless, except around it's borders, where I found myself gazing out through very delicate pastel shades.

When my curiosity was satisfied, I automatically drifted out of it again. I seemed to spend quite some time deep in the water with her, during which no words were spoken. It felt like a sacred togetherness. At the end of it I realised that I knew what she was. One needs to remember that at the first visitation, I did not believe that mermaids even existed, and had consequently never considered what sort of an existence they might have. The first step had been to recognise that they were real. I had managed that with their help, but I was still left not knowing what reality they belonged to. Could it be some other planet? What dimension were they living in? What did they do, or what was their purpose? There is still an enormous amount that I have to learn about them, but after this last meeting in the water, I felt that they are like fairies, like water nature spirits, who help look after the fish. They exist now, today, but are only as visible as the land fairies. One might describe them as sea spirits.

This leads so naturally into the fairy realm, that the next chapter will just have to be about fairies.

Chapter 27
Fairies

13/11/90

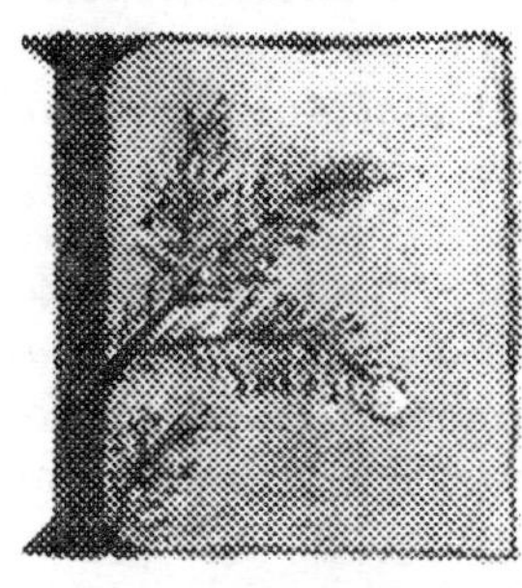

t was a pleasant November afternoon, so I decided that it was a good opportunity to go outside, and do some tidying up in my garden. There was plenty to do, and one of my major tasks seemed to be pulling out the nasturtiums. I had only ever planted these once in my garden, and that was about five years previously. Although they die off each winter with the frost, they leave behind them plenty of seeds, enabling them to reappear in large quantities every following summer. This year they were particularly abundant, and although the frost had still not reached them, their habit of growing all over the other plants, and climbing up everything that they can find, meant that some of the other flowers underneath were unlikely to flower due to lack of light. Therefore, I wanted to get them out, and throw them away as soon as possible, and preferably on this pleasant afternoon while it was still a pleasure to be out, as one did not have to put up with getting frozen while working. The leaves of the little flowers underneath were looking rather yellow and small, but I knew that with their light supply renewed, they would soon improve. Finally everything looked tidy, and I went indoors.

That evening, I was not too surprised to see the nasturtium plants during my meditation. It often happens that the weeds or plants that I have removed will visit me sooner or later. At first I used to feel that I was being haunted or tormented by them, because I had murdered them. Later I realised that they were often feeling rather lost and confused, so I would talk to them. I would thank them for their short lives on this planet in which they had helped improve the air for everybody else by taking in carbon-dioxide and breathing out oxygen during photosynthesis, but then I would explain that I was trying to grow something else in my garden, and that their place was somewhere else on the planet at the moment, in a field, or on a common, or some patch of wild uncultivated ground where they could add to the richness of the flora. However, I would go on, now that I have taken you out of the earth, it would be best for you to leave your physical forms as soon as possible, and join the group plant consciousness to evolve further in what ever way seems best. Return to the place of light where plants go, I would advise them. Usually that was the end of it, and they would leave.

With the nasturtium plants it was different. I was just about to give them their usual little talk to help them on their way, when right in the centre of the most robust specimen, (I knew exactly which one it was), there appeared a little fairy. This was not what I was prepared for! I live on the edge of a town, a nice quiet area, but definitely not part of the countryside. I had heard or read somewhere, that fairies or nature spirits seldom venture into towns, because the atmosphere is so polluted, and the vibrations simply are not suitable for fairy life, so the plants have to manage on their own. That is what I had learnt.

It was obvious that this fairy did not understand why I had chosen to interfere with her little world, and pull out the plants before their time. I explained it all to her, and asked her if she would like to look after a rather young and delicate heather plant that I was particularly fond of. Although I was sitting on the floor in my house out of sight of the heather, it was easy to explain which plant I meant just by thinking about it, which created the picture in my mind for the fairy to see. I was feeling too upset about having destroyed her kingdom to try and see whether or not she accepted my suggestion.

Two nights later, during meditation, I reconnected with her, and decided to ask if she had moved to the heather or not. She showed me the heather this time, and drew my attention to a drop of dew hanging from one of its little branches. This dew drop was full of the most beautiful colours. I felt that her consciousness was in it. Then she showed me how she was drawing up energy from the earth into the heather. I thanked her. A few days later when I was outside in my garden, I noticed that the heather was looking much more vital.

22/11/90

"Thanks-giving Day" in the States. I learnt that from Linda Tellington-Jones's telephone answering machine. As usual it was not straight forward trying to get hold of her. Nevertheless, I finally made it, and was able to answer her post card which I had had for some time, and in addition ask a few questions. For some reason she started talking about fairies, and told me about a really beautiful experience that she had had with them.

In exchange, I told her about this little fairy who was looking after my heather. Linda was moved by this, and pointed out how wonderful it was to communicate with them, as it helped to avoid misunderstandings. "After all", she said, "your little fairy was upset, because she did not understand why you had destroyed her world".

When you consider that most of humanity does not even believe in fairies, the amount of untold damage that we do to our relationships with the other kingdoms is so great that we cannot conceive it. No wonder it is thought that they seldom live in towns.

Later that evening, I decided to save myself some time, by lying in my epsom salt bath, (good for aching muscles after a hard physical day, but depleting if done too often I find), and meditating at the same time. It saved finding separate time for each. As soon as I began to tune in, I heard the words "Fairy Queen", and there was a picture at the same time of an enormous fairy. She had dark hair, and was dressed in white. She was not quite in the bath with me. I suppose that there was not room, but she was almost in it. She held a shining wand with which she drew a circle in the air, not much more than a foot across. The circle was made of silvery light, and had about twelve small twinkling stars spaced around its circumference. She did not say anything about it, but I am sure that I have heard the expression "fairy ring" at some time.

Then she spoke;

> "We were with you by the telephone tonight.
> We listened,
> We approved.
> We thank both of you, and also many others of whom you are not aware, who think and act as you do."

I thanked and acknowledged her. I always find this type of communication extremely moving.

Chapter 28

Galisteo

As I continued working on my book, filling out where necessary, and putting together new material as well, I began to get the feeling that it would be worthwhile to work again with the Light Institute, just in case there were any more undiscovered blocks that could thwart my efforts to get the book published. The previous sessions in Weggis had been so transforming as far as my book was concerned, that to fail now, and after I had put so much more work into it, was unthinkable. For that reason, although it seemed a little soon after the first time, I decided to plan a trip to Galisteo, the home of the Light Institute, in January 1991.

I found this plan to be dual purpose. It not only had a value for the development of the book and me, it also gave me a deadline for completing it. I felt that I could not ask for advice or opinions on something that had only partially manifested, so it would have to be finished (for the second time) before I left for the States. I work better with a little pressure, and was so afraid that I would not manage my self-imposed finishing date, that I actually completed it early. This meant that when a friend of mine invited me over for a meal, knowing that her friend, whom I knew would also be there, was quite good at drawing rabbits amongst other things, I took the manuscript with me, so that I could ask if there was any chance of some illustrations. He refused, because he said that it was much too time consuming, but both of them wanted to have a look at the book. I fetched it in from my car, but the whole of the time that either of them was looking at it, I kept on trying to direct them past the introduction to its proper content. Both of them seemed much more interested in reading about all the dreadful things that happened in my past life, than finding out what the animals said. I was so relieved when they handed it back to me, but I had made a very important discovery.

I was really afraid of sharing my darker secrets with other people. It showed me that I was still unable to accept that possibly people could both love and accept me, and know all about me at the same time. I could only believe that it was either/or. Surely I would lose my credibility as a person if my past were to become known. At last I had learnt to write it all down (thanks to the work at Weggis), but the prospect of letting anyone read what I had written sent large quantities of adrenalin racing round my body. Galisteo was no longer something I was doing just in case there was a block somewhere, it had overnight become something essential.

I had finished the book on 29th. December, and had gone out to dinner searching for an illustrator the following evening. Only two days later on 1st. January, I was to find one.

I was meditating. I opened myself enough to look and see if anything other than me was there. I saw many paint-brushes, all shapes and sizes. In addition, what looked like an artist's pen for outlining was shown. These were displayed with a watercolour paint-box, which was open, and had a lovely selection of bright and varied colours. In front of all this sat a grey rabbit looking at them. *Over his shoulder he informed me, "I'll show you how to* draw those things. I'll help you".

The truth dawned on me that I was to be the illustrator. I had not touched water colours since I was seventeen, and had never been good at drawing things, but I had enjoyed trying.

This latest instruction for me revealed that it was not an artist who would be the third person to work closely with the book, as it seemed that I was to be the artist. (The first and worst rabbit-trained artist on Planet Earth, I wondered? Anyway, it would be fun and a challenge.)

On January 8th. I left for Santa Fe where I would be staying at the Nizhoni Institute during the workshop. This one was also called “Sense of Success”, but without the same slant on business people. It was more about having success on all levels in life. Staying at the “Nizhoni School for Global Consciousness” (Nizhoni Institute), we were driven out to the Light Institute at Galisteo for our sessions.

I was reassured during one of my sessions, when I discovered that I had had a previous life as a monk in which I had done beautiful illuminated lettering, and also wrote philosophy a bit as a result of my studies of other peoples’ works. That was the good news. The bad news was that he/I had a real horror of anyone ever seeing his/my work due to great fear of criticism, and inability to accept help. Clearly I still had these tendencies in my personality, so the session was necessary to uncover and release this behaviour pattern.

In another life, when I was a woman, I had very close contact with nature. Some of my experiences were very similar to those of Michael Roads in his present lifetime, which he describes in his book “*Journey into Nature*”. My experiences were a little different, but when I re-experienced them at the Light Institute, it helped to validate Michael’s story for me.

As a small child, I had spent much of my time in the forest, and came to know and make friends with the forest animals. Some of the deer were quite tame, and I delighted in bringing them their favourite herbs, grasses, and flowers to eat. I was really close to them, and understood their language. Later in my life, after various events had alienated me from people, while I was out in the forest, something like a shaft of light came down and entered into my body. After this, my perception was much greater. I was able to experience two dimensions at once. I could see the energies around me, the life force, and the nature spirits, or the ‘deva kingdom’ as it is also known. This included little twinkling fairy lights in the grass. Seen in this way, nature was almost unbelievably beautiful. I felt her moods, or those of the forest such as joy and sorrow. When there was a change of mood, I felt it before it arrived. It was as though I had psychic antennae with which I could reach out for some distance. I was aware of latent energy at the base of my spine. Nature's energy rippled through my body, and I felt this golden light which was funnelled from above down through the crown chakra, until it filled my entire physical form.

I will now tell the story of my death in this lifetime, because I found the smoothness of the leaving of Earth's reality for another so fascinating.

I had not been happy for some time. Of course I loved the forest, but due to my unusual psychic ability, I was very lonely. One day during a really powerful electrical storm I went out into the forest to be alone with nature. As I was standing beside my favourite oak tree, I felt that the tree had a gift for me. I knew instinctively that it was something I wanted, so I laid my hand on the trunk of the tree to receive. As the lightening struck, and came down the tree, I too was gone in a flash. My physical body fell to the ground in flames, and as I was left standing looking down at it burning at my feet, I saw that the spirit of the oak tree was starting to rise upwards leaving behind its physical self being devoured by the flames. I sensed that it was time for me to depart as well, so I started to drift upwards with the tree spirit. We floated up together through all of the fury of the storm. The reality of the storm began to fade, and as it fell away like a falling curtain, I found myself in another place. I was no longer aware of the tree spirit, but this place was very still, and very quiet. There was a soft golden light, and I was in a garden full of summer flowers. As I lay there on a comfortable couch, there was a beautiful young man standing beside me gently stroking my head who said to me, "Sleep and rest", and I did.

I have noticed that the nature of one's death seems to vary just as much as the different lives do.

As well as re-experiencing many lives as a woman. I worked my way through various lives as a selection of awful men. These were rather slow coming up due to the resistance of my emotional body. During my last session, I had a very strong experience after death of really hating my masculine energy, and not wanting anything more to do with men or their energy. I had spent my life as a really macho man killing and maiming other people in a very callous way. Afterwards when my eyes were opened to how cruel I had been, unable to forgive myself, and believing that if I had been a woman I would not have been so awful, there followed this almost total rejection of anything male. Although partially tamed, much of this dislike of male energy was still with me in this life as Helena, but I had not been aware of it, for it was hidden deep in my subconscious until this and other lives as a man came up.

I had to learn to let the judgement go. I had to understand that the purpose of that life had been to help me understand and not judge men who behaved as badly as I had. After all, I had now seen it from the inside, and received an understanding of how and why someone, having blocked out his feminine feeling intuitive side in order to live up to what he saw as an acceptable image for a man in his situation, could be so violent and unfeeling. I needed to realise that the difference between sexes was an illusion. It is only on a physical level where there is a difference. Spirits don't have a sex. This illustrates yet another of the perils of identifying with the identity of any particular lifetime. It encourages people to believe that they are either a man or a women, instead of realising that we are all both and neither at the same time, depending on how you look at it.

Meanwhile, the animals had not been far away, and who should wish to speak to me, if it was not the grey rabbit.

"This session is so important, because half of us are male, and you work with us also." I had not thought of that, but it was certainly an undeniable truth.

Moments later some dolphins arrived, and there was also a whale with them. One of the dolphins said to me, "It was difficult for us to visit you while you had reservations about male energy. Although we understood, because of our evolvement level we were more sensitive to your condition than the other animals. It is very important to put this in the end of your book". The dolphin came closer, and as it gently nudged my neck with its nose, I stroked its back with my hand. Sadly for me it was necessary to leave the animals at this point in order to continue working on past lives.

This communication reminded me of another that I had had on the preceding 12th. of December. I had been reading the chapter about dolphins in Michael Roads's book "Journey into Nature", which I had found fascinating, and it taught me a lot. This, no doubt, had prepared me for what happened when I sat down to meditate. A dolphin came and swam around me. "You have never been to see me before!", I told it with an air of reproach. "You were not ready for us", it explained, although it said nothing about why not. Then I saw a mixture of dolphins and seals and other fish swimming around me.

Putting my experiences together, I was able to understand why each one of us owes it to ourselves and all of creation to get ourselves as clear and sorted out as possible. Helped by the rabbit and the dolphin, I could see how working on ourselves is an aid to re-integration with the rest of consciousness, thus adding to the capacity of it for good. Thanks to the animals I was experiencing this coming together on a personal level.

The Third Person

As I mentioned in the chapter entitled "AFRICA", when the elephants told me that there were to be three people involved in producing this book, I already knew of two of them, that was Linda and myself, but the third one was to remain for a further thirteen months a mystery to me.

Now in January of 1991, thirteen months later, as I gathered together the relevant pages of my book to photocopy and pass on to Chris Griscom, so that if I had written anything that she felt was inaccurate about her or the Light Institute, then I could change it, I experienced a curious intuitive feeling that something more than just having a few pages checked over was going to come out of this. It is an interesting point, that I noticed afterwards that I had accidentally given her more pages to look at than necessary, so she gained a little greater insight into the nature of it than I had planned.

The day Chris returned those few pages to me, with some helpful suggestions pencilled in the margins here and there, she made me an offer. "If you would like me to write a little preface for it, I would be willing to do that." The feeling that this could be the third person had been gaining strength inside me over the preceding few days, and when I heard this, I knew. "I accept. Thank you very much", was my spontaneous reply. What ever happened to my usual indecision and hesitancy? A strong inner knowing told me that it was right. I had not tried to choose a third person at this time, for I felt that either I would know, or else the animals would tell me who, when it was necessary to know.

Clearly I needed to go home and do some more work on it, so the time was not yet come for anyone to actually write anything for me, but I felt greatly encouraged when I knew that this support was coming to me.

Chapter 29
Difficult Work and More Messages

Difficult Work

n my return from Galisteo, I felt that it was important to follow the advice given to me by two different friends quite independently of each other, and this was to put my book into a "word processor". I had never heard of such a thing, but I was assured that it saved a great deal of work, facilitated better presentation, and was really the only way to write books. I have always thought that good presentation was important, especially if one is trying to sell something. My experience in the horse world had taught me that. Then there was this point about saving work, which had a very strong appeal to my lazy streak, quite apart from saving work meaning more time available for something else, and better use of time available. Therefore, as soon as I could after my return home, I set out on a shopping expedition to try and find a word processor. What ever it cost, I felt that I had to have one. My mission justified anything.

When I arrived at the shop, the salesman was quick to make the assessment that I needed a simple machine. Then he realised that he had just sold the simplest model half an hour previously, and it could be a long wait for another. So between us we decided that I had better have the next one up in the price range, which, although it was more complicated to operate, had the advantage that its print was much easier to read. I thought that this was important, because what publisher wants to struggle through the unclear hard-to-read script of an unknown author. I was horrified to see how much space it was going to take up in my small house, but I thought that as I had to have one, and that as I did not know how to shrink it, I would have to put up with it the size that it was. As I left the shop, I asked, "It does have a manual of instructions with it I suppose?" On receiving an affirmative, I thought that all would be well.

As it was too big for me too carry home, one of the salesmen delivered it that evening. Moments afterwards, I stretched out my hands to pick up the largest looking bit, and jumped back in alarm. I felt this dreadful tingling in my hand as I came into contact with the machine's electro-magnetic field. It was not even plugged in, but to me it was like having an electric shock. I summoned up all my courage, and in spite of its electro-magnetic field, I managed to carry it upstairs to my work room, although I did wish that I did not have to get quite so close to it. There were other shocks to follow. I had the first one when I finally located the manual of instructions at the bottom of one of the packing boxes. I was expecting a little leaflet, at the very most something a fairly slow person might manage in half an hour. This one had 623 pages! The instructions for setting up the printer were in a separate book! I sank down into the nearest chair to recover from this discovery.

While I was sitting there, I suddenly noticed that the part known as the "monitor unit" had "Personal Computer Word Processor" written on it. "Computer!!", I thought to myself filled with horror. I had always known that I was quite definitely not of a suitable mentality to cope with a computer. I was not equipped with the right kind of brain for it, and I had even heard of people losing their books in computers. I was certain that if I had known that I was buying a computer, I would never have done so, but nobody had said anything about a computer, and I thought that it was just a harmless thing called a "word processor" that I was getting. That altered nothing now. There it was complete with the formidable book of instructions, paid for, and sitting on top of my work table in front of me, and me on the back of my chair trying to keep as far away as possible from its electro-magnetic field. "I will have to make friends with this somehow", I thought to myself. "After all, it is going to do some wonderful work for me." Over the next ten days, I spent as much time as possible when I was not with the horses trying to learn how to master it, and come to terms with its presence in my house. Twice during that period I telephoned the salesman, first to tell him the I thought the attachments were at fault, and later to ask if he would please replace the printer, as I had definitely been sold one that was faulty. He was very patient with me, and eventually by following his advice given over the telephone, I discovered that actually there was nothing wrong with any of the equipment, only Helena was not working properly.

Having no previous training in computers, I sooner or later encountered almost every possible problem. I could never remember what it was that had finally after a hard struggle made it work yesterday. Eventually the day arrived when I found that I felt ready to "risk" putting my book into it for editing, adding to, and then printing. It has a "spelling check", and when I saw how many words I had spelt wrongly, I began to understand why my friends thought I needed a word processor. When I want to spell something, I not only cannot remember how it should be spelt, I can't even remember how I spelt it two sentences ago.

If you are feeling totally mystified to find so much about my experiences with a computer in a book of this type, then let me explain. I think it is very important. I feel that if I can learn through perseverance to do these things in order to achieve the goal of producing a book nicely, then so could almost anybody. I was not a suitable candidate for it, and yet I am using the thing. I feel more comfortable meditating than working with a computer, but it serves me for which I am grateful. Now I am hoping that perhaps someone who has something wonderful that perhaps they would like to share with the rest of us in a book, but feels that writing, spelling, and using computers is too far beyond them, will feel so encouraged that they will reconsider the project, and be rewarded by the joy of creation.

More Messages

Now I am moving back in time a little, in order to include that which came to me around Christmas and the New Year. There had been countless showings on the television of fairy stories, mermaid stories, all kinds of children's "make-believe" stories, and, not least, dramatisations of Beatrix Potter's children's animal stories. Beyond doubt, the atmosphere was clogged up with the thought forms from these programmes, and I could not avoid them impinging on my consciousness during meditation. As I sat there looking at Peter Rabbit, and all his little friends, I heard a voice belonging to none of them which told me that those who create these appealing little animal characters, and those who fill the media with such stories are performing their own type of spiritual work. Children are left feeling warmly towards animals, (almost always), and the possible reality of mermaids, fairies, and unicorns, for example, is kept alive in people's minds. Although it is only the 'idea' that they are real, and not the 'belief', it nonetheless provides a foundation on which can be built a future philosophy or expansion of consciousness for mankind.

Personally, I am very curious to know more about unicorns. I had discounted them as a possible reality until early in December 1990, when during my meditation at home, I saw the head, neck, and shoulders of a unicorn. I had no doubt that the picture was real, but I did think that perhaps it looked a bit inanimate, and I wondered if maybe this was just a passing thought form. A few days later when not meditating, I saw another one, or the same one. It looked the same, and passed across my field of vision from right to left. The big difference this time was that it appeared to have life! As it passed me, I saw the eyes turn, and it took a good look at me, so that I felt that it was carefully observing my reaction to its presence. I felt no fear, and I was very interested.

After Galisteo, having done so much work during my sessions on the masculine and female energies present in all of us, I could not help wondering (for the umpteenth time) if maybe it would be a good idea to have a relationship with a man. I was not totally happy about the idea, because even if I successfully manifested that into my life, perhaps it would lead me away from my mission and proper work which was my main purpose for being here. I saw it as potentially taking me away from the spiritual side of my life that I was trying to nurture. Secondly, perhaps if I fell in love, and gave everything up for that, when three months later we fell "out of love", I would just collapse in a heap somewhere having lost everything. These thoughts are probably what brought about the following brief but beautiful meditation.

On 21st. January, to my delight, there came a mermaid to see me. We were sitting on the ocean floor, the mermaid seated on a small rock, and I was just hovering a few yards away from her. She sent me a large pink bubble through the water. I received it joyfully, and automatically wished to respond by sending a bubble to her. As my bubble for her left me, I saw that it was pale blue. "Wear it!", she commanded, as I clasped the pink bubble with my hands. I stepped inside as bidden, and noticed that she was wearing the blue one that I had sent her. We drifted towards each other, and then with the two bubbles pressed up against one another, and with our arms extended slightly forwards and sideways, we managed to hold hands, thus bringing the pink and blue bubbles even closer together.

At this point, although I remained holding hands, a part of my consciousness moved away, so that I could watch what was happening from outside of the bubbles from three or four yards away. Something remarkable started to take place. On the sides where the bubbles were pressed against each other, they began to merge like two cells becoming one. It was never a total merging, but half of each was transformed into a beautiful shade of lilac where the pink and the blue mixed, while half remained the original colour. The mermaid explained to me that this was what a relationship could be like as the masculine (blue) energy, and the feminine (pink) energy came together, a truly spiritual energy. Lilac to me is the colour of spirituality. Yet one saw that both energies retained some of their original colour and identity.

I think it is only possible for a mermaid to bring me such wonderful things because they are so connected to the Source from which we all come, and to which we all return.

From the Primates

When I spoke to Linda T.-J. in February, she asked me if I would connect with the higher-consciousness of the primates, and ask what was coming from them, as she felt that there might be something exciting, because she was currently working with chimps who had previously been in a research laboratory. I agreed, but after I had thought about it, I felt uneasy about just sitting down and calling them. I had a sense of wrong timing, and I knew that both I and the environment had to be just right for the best results. The animals had always known exactly when to come before, so I decided to wait for a while, and see if they would appear in their own time. I asked no questions.

On 2nd. March, I sat down rather later than usual to meditate before going to bed, having first settled body and mind with half an hour's dancing to music in the candle light. Mostly it was just a silent, still meditation, but knowing that in spite of the cease-fire in the Gulf, there was still great need and misery there, I opened up my crown chakra like a wide angle camera lens in order to draw in as much white light as possible, and then send it out through my body to the Gulf where it was needed. I thought of the trees, and how when they channelled light, they too were very wide open at the top.

I had only been doing this for a moment or two, when I thought to myself "Something is happening." I went on "full alert". I was looking at the face of a medium sized monkey. This was no passing thought form, for as I watched it, slowly the rest of its body came into view. This was immediately followed by the appearance of four or five other monkeys. (Incidently, as I know nothing about primates, I use words like 'monkey' and 'chimp' to mean exactly the same thing.) These monkeys were living in captivity, but they had been given a lot of things to play with, and were very busy. One of them had a whistle, the type which uncurls when you blow it, and it was clearly delighted with this toy, as it ran around blowing it vigorously. All of them were amusing themselves with something, and were very entertaining to watch.

The next development was seeing humans watching them. The people were visibly moved. I realised that some of these primates have incredibly appealing faces. The people, however, were not the normal cross-section of society that one expects to see. Some of them had behavioural problems, or were 'learning disabled'. Some were very withdrawn with emotional difficulties, and were unable to relate to other people properly, but showed such interest in the totally uninhibited chimps that they were starting to dare to come out of themselves a little. The animals were literally healing the people.

"You rehabilitate us, and we will rehabilitate you", said one of them.

The scene changed, and I saw the back view of a large black gorilla pouring over a map of the World. With a forefinger he indicated two areas on it. One was in the rain forests around the Amazon in South America, and the other was in Australia. When he turned round, I saw that he was enjoying a half peeled banana. Nonetheless, without appearing to have to empty his mouth first, he was able to tell me,

"We have a plan For helping man."

The only condition for this to work, he told me, was that we should co-operate with them. Nothing more specific than this was given, but it shines out like a bright ray of hope.

Chapter 30

The Wisdom of Consciousness

hen I went to Switzerland to work with The Light Institute of Galisteo, one of the ways that I had justified it to myself was that it would be a good idea to go and satisfy my curiosity, (perhaps I should say 'burning' curiosity) and then I would not have to spend the rest of my life wondering what it would have been like and so forth. I never imagined repeating the experience. Then I had unexpectedly (as far as I was concerned) visited Galisteo the following January for more, and amazed myself still further by returning again the following April to join in the "Spirituality Workshop". Once again, I was going where my heart led me, and the experience was rich.

For me consciousness is that magic something which governs the movements of universes, and all that is. To me it means the god-energy that is present in everything, and which is conscious of itself.

Sometimes in meditation one connects with the consciousness of the animals, other times with the plant kingdom, other times with the mineral kingdom, other times with the consciousness of one's own higher self, or with other planets and their inhabitants, or even in so-called "past life" sessions with the awareness and knowledge gained by one's own soul during other incarnations, be they on this planet or elsewhere. It is this type of experience that

I wish to share. As usual, a number of my "bad" lives came up, which was useful, as we could clear them out, but two of the others have more relevance to this book.

The first one that I find interesting is the tale of a female psychic. It took place in a warm dry climate, where the ground was covered with a reddish-brown sand. As was usual, like my friends, I normally dressed in black, and my skin was a sun-tanned brown. I would estimate that it was at least a few hundred years ago, but the intriguing thing to me was, that I made full use of my psychic gifts in a spiritual way without getting locked up, becoming friendless, being burnt at the stake as a witch, or doing anything to attract undesired attention to myself.

I found myself standing beside an urn filled with water. I had a good understanding of water, and I knew that water from different places had different energies in it. I could feel the energy in the trees, and was particularly aware of moving energy, auras, and subtle bodies. I would extend my own aura like an antenna, so that I could feel other energies interacting with mine. Clairvoyantly, I would watch the energy moving up and down the trees, and I knew that this energy which I was perceiving was behind creation. This was God. I observed that energy had its own intelligence, and that some could be destructive. Where there had been corruption, I saw polluted energy fields which were dark and heavy. They could be helped by sending them light to transmute the darkness. I saw how when people who were unaware of it moved into these places, the bad energy polluted them. Only those with really strong light auras were able to pass through unaffected. Where there had been violence and malicious thought, the energy field became so heavy and dense that it almost resembled a thick soup. Therefore I understood the importance of keeping one's own thoughts pure.

I had a few close women friends, and sometimes we would go out in a group, varying from two to six of us, to work on cleansing the atmosphere, to move these dark energies, and also to help the spirits trapped in these places to find the light. We would draw the light into our own bodies through the crown chakra, and then direct it out from the solar plexus into the darkness, just very gently at first, as the spirits we were helping were not accustomed to light, and we did not wish to dazzle them, or scare them. When the spirits were ready to leave, angels came and helped to guide them away. Sometimes the angels would remain invisible to those they were helping, lest they cause them alarm. Nearly all of my life was dedicated to this work. (Perhaps it was karma for something dreadful that I did in some of my other lives.)

I also wove cloth. This is what my occupation appeared to be as far as most of the people could see. Into the cloth I wove my thought patterns, patterns of light and healing, so that those who made their clothes from my cloth would be uplifted and healed.

My death came as a surprise to me, for I was in good health, and life was going well for me, even though I had reached the age of sixty, which was considered very old. It was both beautiful and simple. I was lying alone on my bed in the darkness of the night, when my little room was filled with light. I saw two angels standing at the door. "It is time for you to come with us now", they called to me. I got up out of my physical body which I left behind lying on the bed, and walked away with the angels, who took me to a beautiful place where I was able to rest.

The second life to be shared was one where my facilitator had asked me to ask my higher self to show me a life where I had succeeded in living my divinity. (Just to keep things in perspective, we did a second life that day, in which I was a woman, to cover rape, incest, repression, and fear with a long drawn out illness and a painful death at the end of it.)

So this time, I found myself as a young man of small stature walking up a hill somewhere in a more southerly country than the British Isles. I was walking a little ahead of a crowd of people who were following me because I was teaching them. My heart felt very light, and I was happy, because I always followed my heart, and therefore I had no regrets to weigh me down. I was pointing things out to the people as we went, teaching them about the sun and the moon and the stars. Sometimes in the evenings we lit a fire and sat around it under the night sky, while I taught them what I knew. My followers were also my friends,and we worked together making maps of the stars. I was an astrologer, which involved spending much time doing research work, and making written records of my findings.

I had a lot of joy, which I was able to pass on to the people around me.

I was aware that the stars and planets all had different energies, and I was able to feel which of them was affecting the earth at the time. As a natural psychic, I made trips out of my body to connect more closely with the individual planets, especially Venus, Saturn, the Pleiades, and various others. I would slip out of my body, and travel on a silver line directly to my destination. I remained very conscious during these trips, and was therefore able to bring back with me all of the memories and information.

(At this point in my session, my facilitator asked me to go on one of those trips. It did not turn out how I expected!)

The planet that I travelled to had an energy with a very strong orange colour. I felt as I arrived that it had a strong pull on the chakras from the solar plexus downwards, and I felt its energy pulsating through the whole of me, and I also felt some of it affecting my head and the higher chakras, but the colours were only present lower down in my body, everything from red through to yellow. I remarked that it was a strange energy. It was very powerful, with a strong effect on the physical body influencing movement and awareness. It was a heavy type of vibration, but not too heavy. I felt that these energies had something to do with reproduction.

When I returned to the earth, I found that I had brought back with me the vibrations and energy of this planet. As I looked around me, I saw that it moved the animal and plant kingdoms to reproduce. Men and animals are drawn towards the appropriate partner by it. I felt the energy in my own body driving me forward through the darkness, until I found myself with a woman in my arms, who later turned out to be the perfect wife. It had manifested for me the ideal partner. She kept the house for me, she was very precious to me, and she provided a loving environment both for us and our children to live in. It seems to me that this is what happens when your heart is pure, and as like attracts like, one allows oneself to be drawn towards a partner on an energy level, instead of just picking the one with blue eyes for example. The only sad event that came up was the death of our youngest child from dysentery, but looking after the other four of them, and my concern for my wife helped me to get through this difficult time.

I suppose that it is not surprising that in a life where I was so consciously connected to the planets, that further contact with them should turn out to be a pre-planned part of that life time. As Helena, however, it took me completely by surprise, when while watching myself as this man going for a night-time stroll up the hill with the intention of looking at my friends in the sky (the moon and the stars) from the hilltop, that I should find a UFO waiting for me half way up the hill. As the man I never hesitated for an instant, but carried on walking, and stepped inside the spaceship as though I did it everyday of my life. The ship left, and suddenly we were outside the dimension of Planet Earth.

The UFO and everything with it was like a very pale yellow and white light. I knew that I could not survive in a human body for long outside the earth's atmosphere, and the space people knew this as well, so almost immediately they gathered round me, and by touching me very lightly they started to transmute my body into something that looked like a light body in which I could comfortably live while I was with them. The vibrations here were faster and lighter than those of the planet with the orange energy, and I felt very content with them. I noticed that there was one area of me that they very carefully did not transmute, and that was the part of me in which was stored my knowledge of the Earth, and what it means to be a human being. Piece by piece I shared this knowledge with the space people. They were interested in learning about emotions and human behaviour.

For my part, I was very fascinated by everything that I found around me. Meanwhile we seemed to have passed from the reality of the ship into their dimension without any well defined moment in which this had happened. We were existing in whatever planetary reality they regarded as their normal environment. These beings had no knowledge of pain or emotions, rather like living just on a mental and intuitive level. Therefore, while I was with them, I felt no pain or even the realisation that I had just left a loving wife and family behind me. This knowledge only returned to me after I had left the space people. That happened after the exchange of knowledge was complete. I had certainly received much from them concerning the dynamics of their reality. When I left them, I rose upwards leaving my space body behind, (it seemed to be simultaneously reabsorbed into the atmosphere) and passed through some bright light arriving in a place where I knew that I was no longer incarnated anywhere. I remembered my wife. I realised that as only a short period of time had passed on the Earth, the conception of time had been quite different for me while I was away from it. Time with the space people was much more elastic, it was outside of time. They moved through time, and in and out of time. It was all much more flexible than on Earth, because there was not any time, and yet all time. Language is barely adequate to describe it.

Meanwhile my children were more or less grown up and ready to manage without us. My wife was missing me, and she was approaching her death. For about five nights running, I contacted her in her sleep in order to prepare her for this. Then something beautiful happened. I arrived at her bedside in my spirit body, took her hand, lifted her up out of her physical body, and, as the silver cord snapped, we departed together. It was a very joyful reunion.

As I lay on the table as Helena, I saw the line of strong white light which still connects me to that reality. I felt the energy from that planet, whichever it is, pulsating powerfully through the whole of my body, and once again experienced the feelings of homesickness, and longing for that which I had left behind. I also saw that I am connected to other places. Many other connecting lines were leading away from my body in different directions, but this shining white one was by far the most powerful. This experience re-enforced for me the validity of my experiences described in chapter six, where an angel took me to another planet during one of George Pratt's meditation classes.

It is clear to me that no part of consciousness is an island. We are all part of a whole, and that recognising this makes that whole stronger on every level. It is also logical that if one part of a universe is sick, then the health of the whole is impaired, which explains so very clearly why enlightened extra-terrestrials are interested in understanding and assisting with the situation on Planet Earth.

At the time when I received the following poem, (February 1988) I was just trying to see if I could channel, and I wrote down the words as they came to me. I understood so much less then than now, that I regarded it as mostly rubbish, but nonetheless filed it away with all my other rubbish! Now I find it an appropriate ending for this book. I no longer see it as rubbish, but regard it as something useful.

A Poem My Parting Gift

Oh star! I wonder what you are,
How calm and bright and far,
I seem to sense a twinkling eye
Come glistening through the sky.

Oh never let me doubt the truth
That seems to fade with youth,
But let me see with clarity
The truth by me so sought.

There was a time, yes once I thought
I knew enough of life,
But now I see how time has brought
An age of endless strife.

It will not do to go on through
This life, and disregard
The needs of others unfulfilled,
Although it may seem hard.

And so you shining twinkling star
That shares this universe,
Send wisdom to us, as we are
Of you, and you of us.

FREE CATALOGUE

Capall Bann is owned and run by people actively involved in many of the areas in which we publish. A detailed illustrated catalogue is available on request, SAE or International Postal Coupon appreciated. **Titles can be ordered direct from Capall Bann, post free in the UK** (cheque or PO with order) or from good bookshops and specialist outlets.
Do contact us for details on the latest releases at: **Capall Bann Publishing, Freshfields, Chieveley, Berks, RG20 8TF.** Titles include:

A Breath Behind Time, Terri Hector
Auguries and Omens - The Magical Lore of Birds, Yvonne Aburrow
Between Earth and Sky, Julia Day
Caer Sidhe - Celtic Astrology and Astronomy, Vol 1, Michael Bayley
Caer Sidhe - Celtic Astrology and Astronomy, Vol 2 M Bayley
Cat's Company, Ann Walker
Celtic Lore & Druidic Ritual, Rhiannon Ryall
Celtic Saints and the Glastonbury Zodiac, Mary Caine
Crystal Clear - A Guide to Quartz Crystal, Jennifer Dent
Crystal Doorways, Simon & Sue Lilly
Crossing the Borderlines - Guising, Masking & Ritual Animal Disguise, Nigel Pennick
Dragons of the West, Nigel Pennick
Earth Harmony - Places of Power, Holiness & Healing, Nigel Pennick
Enchanted Forest - The Magical Lore of Trees, Yvonne Aburrow
Eternal Priestess, Sage Weston
Everything You Always Wanted To Know About Your Body, But So Far
Nobody's Been Able To Tell You, Chris Thomas & D Baker
Face of the Deep - Healing Body & Soul, Penny Allen
Fairies in the Irish Tradition, Molly Gowen
Familiars - Animal Powers of Britain, Anna Franklin
From Past to Future Life, Dr Roger Webber
Gardening For Wildlife Ron Wilson
Handbook of Fairies, Ronan Coghlan
Healing Book, The, Chris Thomas and Diane Baker
Healing Homes, Jennifer Dent
Healing Journeys, Paul Williamson
Healing Stones, Sue Philips
Herb Craft - Shamanic & Ritual Use of Herbs, Lavender & Franklin
Legend of Robin Hood, The, Richard Rutherford-Moore
Lore of the Sacred Horse, Marion Davies
Magic of Herbs - A Complete Home Herbal, Rhiannon Ryall
Magical Guardians - Exploring the Spirit and Nature of Trees, Philip Heselton
Magical History of the Horse, Janet Farrar & Virginia Russell
Magical Lore of Cats, Marion Davies

Medicine For The Coming Age, Lisa Sand MD
Menopause and the Emotions, Kathleen I Macpherson
Mind Massage - 60 Creative Visualisations, Marlene Maundrill
Mirrors of Magic - Evoking the Spirit of the Dewponds, P Heselton
Mystic Life of Animals, Ann Walker
Patchwork of Magic - Living in a Pagan World, Julia Day
Personal Power, Anna Franklin
Places of Pilgrimage and Healing, Adrian Cooper
Practical Divining, Richard Foord
Practical Meditation, Steve Hounsome
Practical Spirituality, Steve Hounsome
Psychic Self Defence - Real Solutions, Jan Brodie
Real Fairies, David Tame
Romany Tapestry, Michael Houghton
Runic Astrology, Nigel Pennick
Sacred Animals, Gordon MacLellan
Sacred Celtic Animals, Marion Davies, Ill. Simon Rouse
Sacred Dorset - On the Path of the Dragon, Peter Knight
Sacred Nature, Ancient Wisdom & Modern Meanings, A Cooper
Season of Sorcery - On Becoming a Wisewoman, Poppy Palin
Seasonal Magic - Diary of a Village Witch, Paddy Slade
Secret Signs & Sigils, Nigel Pennick
Spirits of the Air, Jaq D Hawkins
Spirits of the Earth, Jaq D Hawkins
Stumbling Through the Undergrowth , Mark Kirwan-Heyhoe
Talking to the Earth, Gordon MacLellan
Taming the Wolf - Full Moon Meditations, Steve Hounsome
Tree: Essence of Healing, Simon & Sue Lilly
Tree: Essence, Spirit & Teacher, Simon & Sue Lilly
Understanding Chaos Magic, Jaq D Hawkins
Vortex - The End of History, Mary Russell
Warp and Weft - In Search of the I-Ching, William de Fancourt
Warriors at the Edge of Time, Jan Fry
Wildwood King , Philip Kane
Wondrous Land - The Faery Faith of Ireland by Dr Kay Mullin
Working With the Merlin, Geoff Hughes
Your Talking Pet, Ann Walker